No Words Posters
one image is enough

Armando Milani

Foreword by
R. Roger Remington

RIT Press
Rochester, New York

for Massimo Vignelli

No Words Posters: one image is enough.
© 2015   Rochester Institute of Technology and Armando Milani
All rights reserved.

Book and cover design by Armando Milani

Published and distributed by:

RIT Press
90 Lomb Memorial Drive
Rochester, NY 14623
http://ritpress.rit.edu

Printed in the U.S.A.

ISBN 978-1-939125-09-5 (print)
ISBN 978-1-939125-10-1 (e-book)

Library of Congress Cataloging-in-Publication Data

Milani, Armando, 1940–
No words posters : one image is enough / Armando Milani.
     pages   cm
   Includes index.
   ISBN 978-1-939125-09-5 (alk. paper) — ISBN 978-1-939125-10-1
(e-book)
   1. Posters--Themes, motives. I. Title.
   NC1815.M55 2015
   741.6′74—dc23
                                           2014045152

The Effectiveness of Non-Verbal Communication

In his book *No Words Posters*, Armando Milani has selectively gathered a personal collection of posters that communicate solely with imagery. He has done extensive research in this special genre of posters and the result mirrors Milani's own rare vision. His outstanding works, such as the cigarette to snake transformation, are in good company in these pages with many other elite graphic designs. Limiting the visual variables in a poster to only imagery, poses a great challenge for the graphic designer. It demands a clear concept and a simple approach. In contrast to the plethora of posters which use text and imagery, the works represented in this book are unique.

We learn from this book that posters without text transcend language barriers and easily communicate archetypical messages in their universality. Milani has discovered a form of "graphic design without borders."

Design theory offers us one way to more deeply appreciate and analyze these images. Seeing many of these posters through a rhetorical lens affords us the opportunity to tap into a powerful communication potential among the subject, the visual concept, the designer and the viewer.
Many of the most effective posters are consciously or intuitively based on obvious rhetorical figures such as analogy, metaphor, ambiguity, hyperbole and others.

For example, Albe Steiner's poster with plants growing in a military helmet shows ambiguity. Mirko Ilić's poster making a hangman's noose from a cord to a computer mouse is an oxymoron. In this context again Milani's poster in which a cigarette transforms into a snake is an understatement of a powerful message to stop smoking. This book is a treasure trove of images in which the designers intuitively signify many rhetorical devices.

Additionally, a useful criterion for poster evaluation was offered many years ago by the great Russian Constructivist designer El Lissitzky who wrote," An effective poster must first seduce the eye and then address the intelligence of the viewer." Because of the singular emphasis on the imagery represented in this book, the posters function very well at "seducing the eye."

The examples in this book, over and over again, provide the reader with a new appreciation of how imagery can have visual impact and then deliver a message with clarity and richness. For these new ways of looking at the world, we need to applaud the mind and vision of Armando Milani.

R. Roger Remington
Vignelli Distinguished
Professor of Design
Rochester Institute of Technology

Introduction

Communication is the exchange of ideas and feelings, and an image is worth a thousand words.

The philosopher Roland Barthes says, "The image always has the last word."

With these concepts in mind, I have collected almost two hundred extraordinary posters from all parts of the world. They reflect the graphic designer's ability to evoke emotion and understanding without using any words because the symbols speak for themselves.

In some cases, with the consent of the designers, we have deleted a few lines of text that were not essential to the meaning of the poster's symbolism.

In the back of this book, you will find the original copy of each poster with its intended description and comments. Finally, there are also short essays about "no words" from some of the included designers.

Many posters are designed by my colleagues in Alliance Graphique International (AGI). Others are by younger graphic designers, winners of various international competitions.

I was pleased to notice that an increasing number of highly creative women graphic designers have emerged over the last years.

The contributors to this book use photography, typography, collages or illustrations. They use a sense of humor, metaphors, or dramatic images to confront the most crucial issues of our time.

These posters represent a variety of periods, styles, countries, and cultures. In their work, the designers set aside established religions and dogma in search of the truth.

They all have a common denominator: the ethical need to improve the quality of our life and of society by encouraging dialogue and reflection about our humanity.

Many posters offer immediate interpretation, but others are more cryptic, and that is their appeal. These images are stimulating, and they capture attention because the viewer is challenged to solve the riddle.

The ground rules of graphic design usually recommend the use of no more than a few basic typefaces. I teach my students these same principles, but in this book I want to show that, sometimes, we can avoid even that. In so doing, our work can reach out and speak to the entire world.

These are silent posters. They offer timeless solutions, not ephemeral fashion.

The purpose of this book is to demonstrate that simplicity and ingenuity are the hallmarks of good and powerful design.

People often ask us: what is the difference between art and graphic design?

In this book, I am showing that sometimes there is no difference.

Armando Milani

Designer
Woody Pirtle

Country
U.S.A.

Year
2001

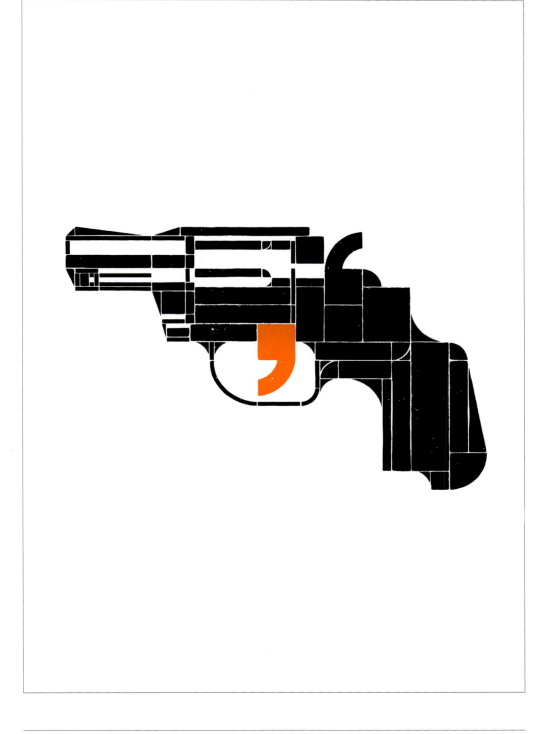

Designer
Stefan Sagmeister
Matthias Ernstberger

Country
U.S.A.

Year
2007

Designer
Albe Steiner

Country
Italy

Year
1962

8

Designer
Luba Lukova

Country
U.S.A

Year
2000

9

Designer
Masuteru Aoba

Country
Japan

Year
1987

10

Designer
Steff Geissbühler

Country
U.S.A.

Year
1984

11

Designer
Shigeo Fukuda

Country
Japan

Year
1980

12

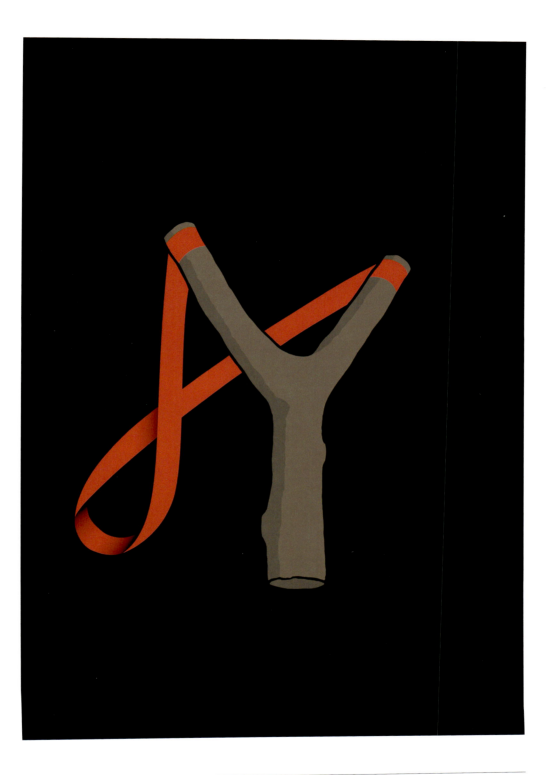

Designer
Chaz Maviyane-Davies

Country
Zimbabwe

Year
2007

13

Designer
Yossi Lemel

Country
Israel

Year
2006

16

Designer
Yossi Lemel

Country
Israel

Year
2006

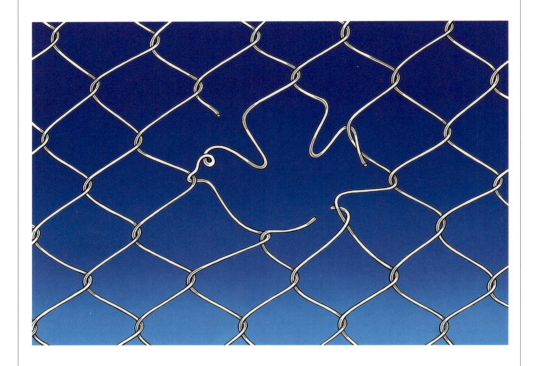

Designer
U. G. Sato

Country
Japan

Year
1978

18

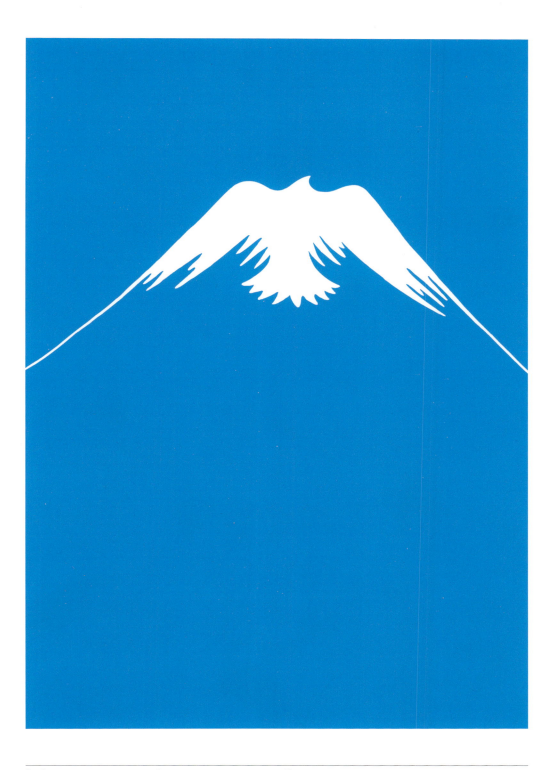

Designer
U.G. Sato

Country
Japan

Year
2008

19

Designer
Yusaku Kamekura

Country
Japan

Year
1983

20

Designer
Federica Marangoni

Country
Italy

Year
2012

21

Designer
Isidro Ferrer

Country
Spain

Year
2003

22

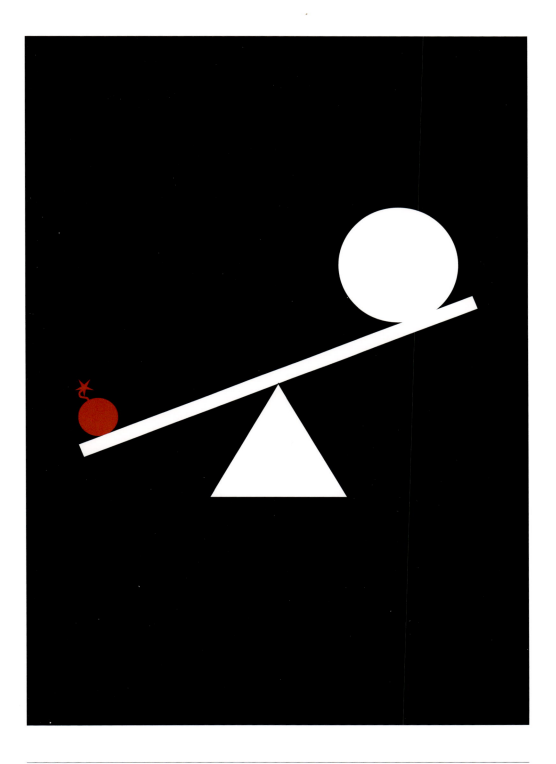

Designer
Armando Milani

Country
Italy

Year
2008

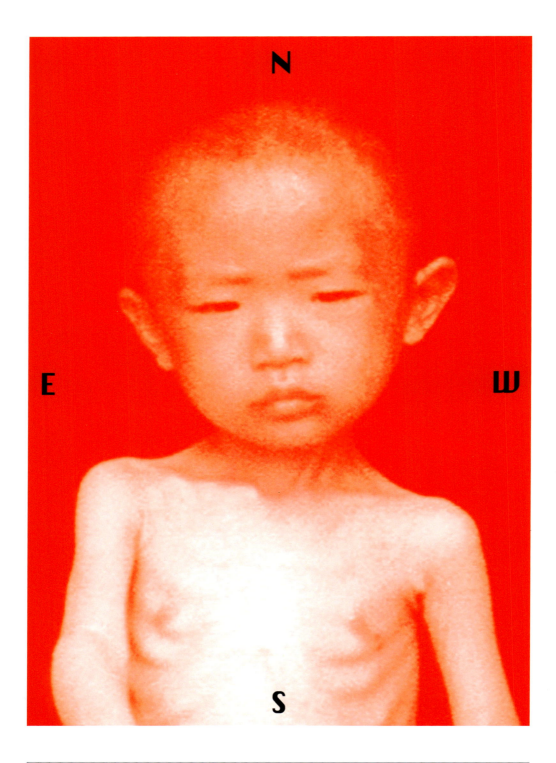

Designer
Uwe Loesch

Country
Germany

Year
2001

24

Designer
B. Martin Pedersen

Country
U.S.A.

Year
1971

25

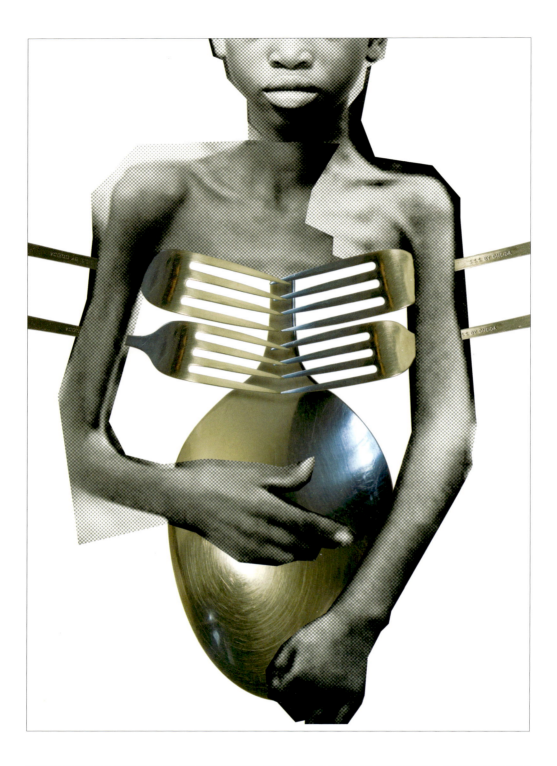

Designer
Chaz Maviyane-Davies

Country
Zimbabwe

Year
2009

26

Designer
Jukka Veistola

Country
Finland

Year
1969

Designer
Jukka Veistola

Country
Finland

Year
1970

Designer
Maciej Urbaniec

Country
Poland

Year
1972

29

Designer
Uwe Loesch

Country
Germany

Year
1989

Designer
Grapus

Country
France

Year
1972
Series 1

31

Designer
Grapus

Country
France

Year
1972
Series 2

32

Designer
Grapus

Country
France

Year
1972
Series 3

33

Designer
Werner Jeker

Country
Switzerland

Year
1989

34

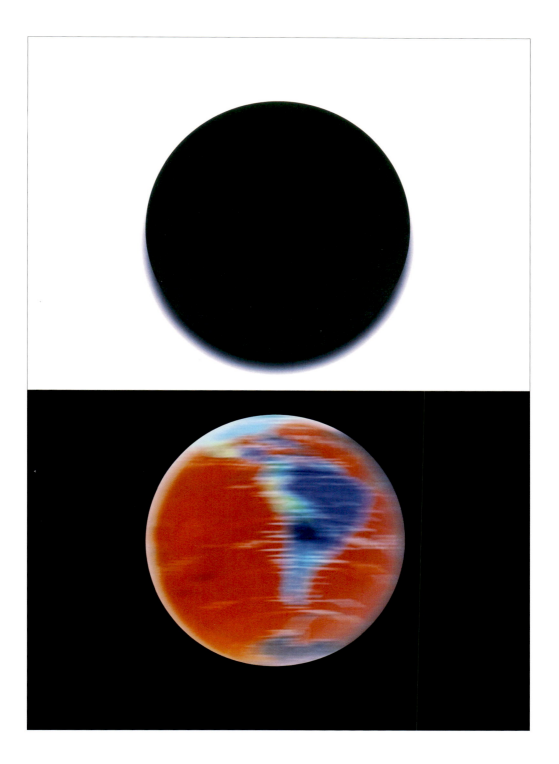

Designer
Werner Jeker

Country
Switzerland

Year
1999

35

Designer
Isidro Ferrer

Country
Spain

Year
2007

Designer
2xGoldstein

Country
Germany

Year
2007

37

Designer
John Rushworth

Country
U.K.

Year
1998

38

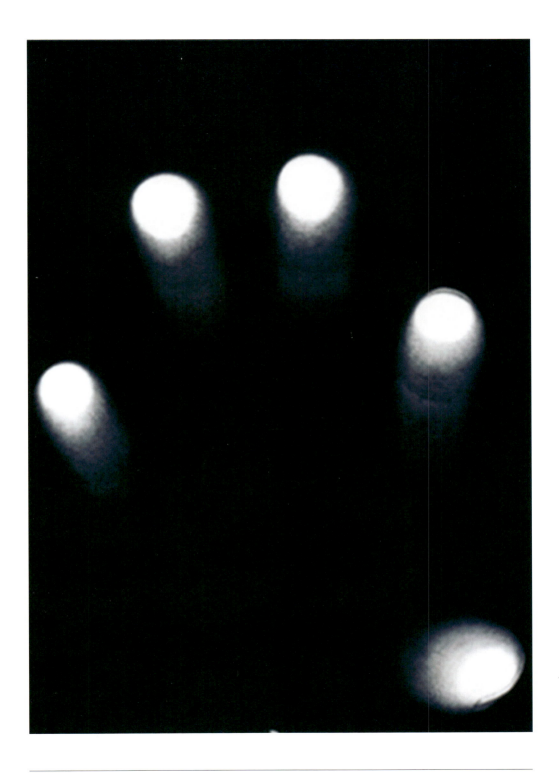

Designer
Koichi Sato

Country
Japan

Year
1996

39

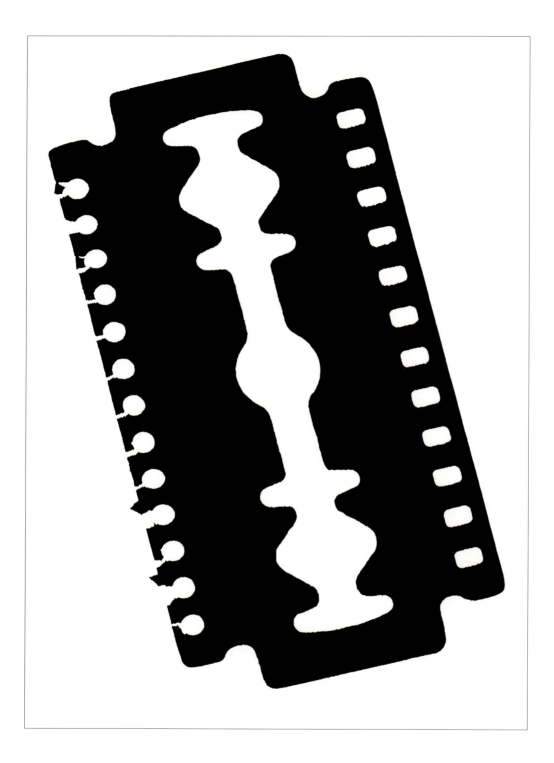

Designer
Kari Piippo

Country
Finland

Year
1990

40

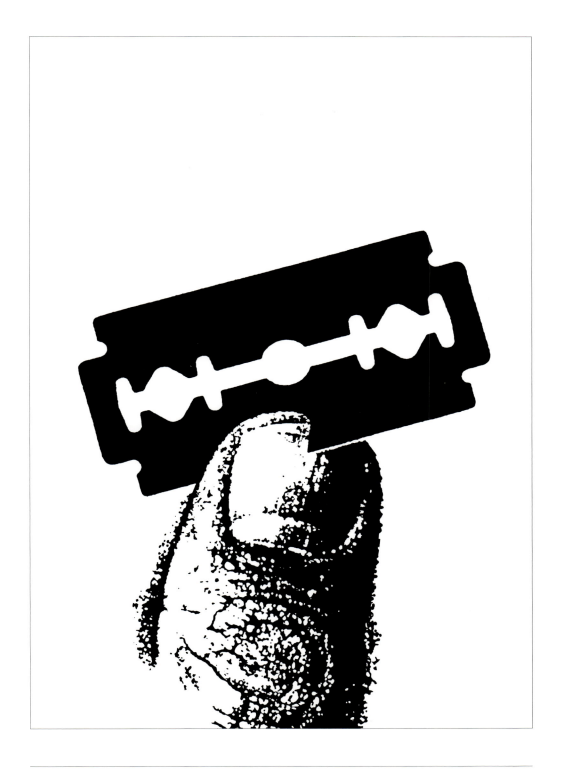

Designer
Stephan Bundi

Country
Switzerland

Year
1985

41

Designer
Fons Hickmann

Country
Germany

Year
1978

Designer
Chatri na Ranong

Country
Australia

Year
2007

Designer
Sergio Olivotti

Country
Italy

Year
2002

44

Designer
Woody Pirtle

Country
U.S.A.

Year
2011

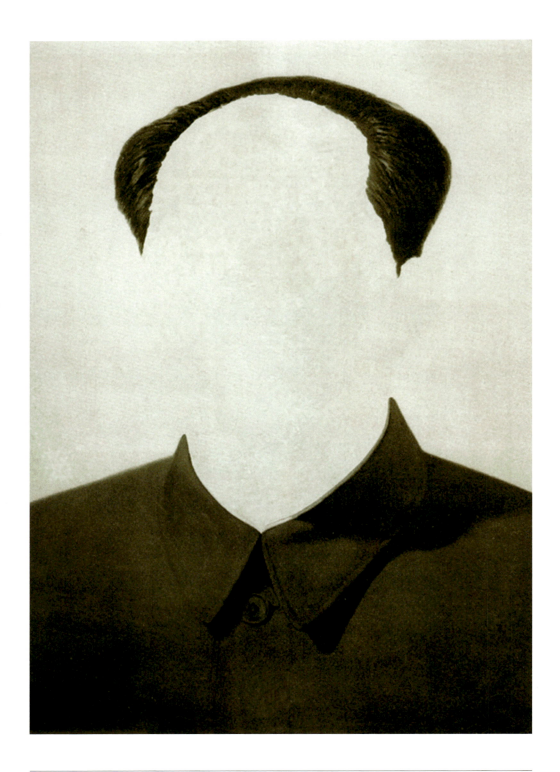

Designer
Jianping He

Country
Germany

Year
1999

46

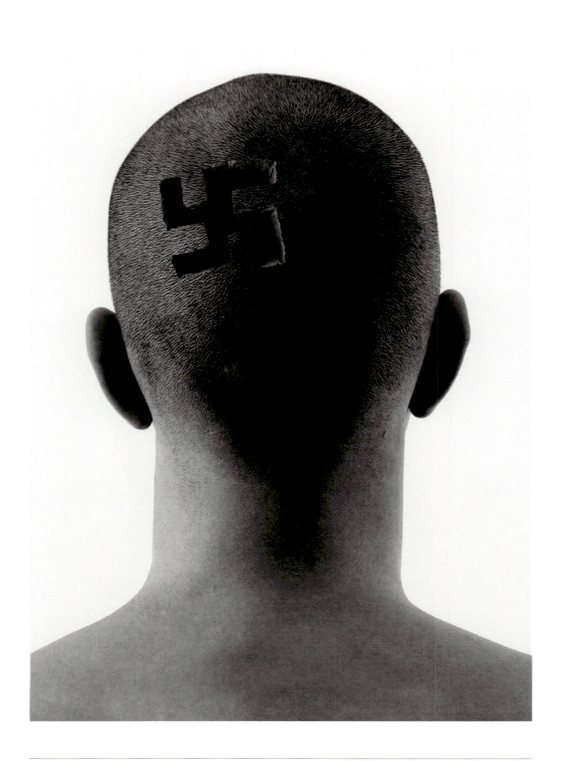

Designer
Jianping He

Country
Germany

Year
2000

47

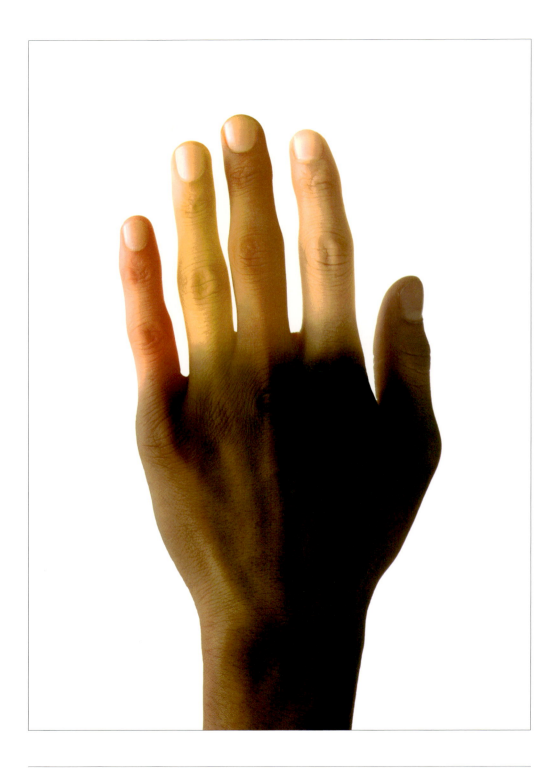

Designer
Milton Glaser

Country
U.S.A.

Year
2005

48

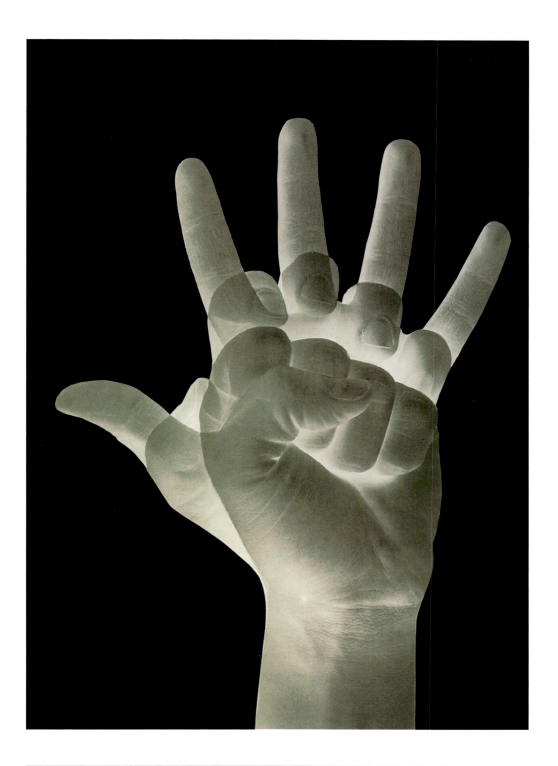

Designer
Armando Milani

Country
Italy

Year
1973

49

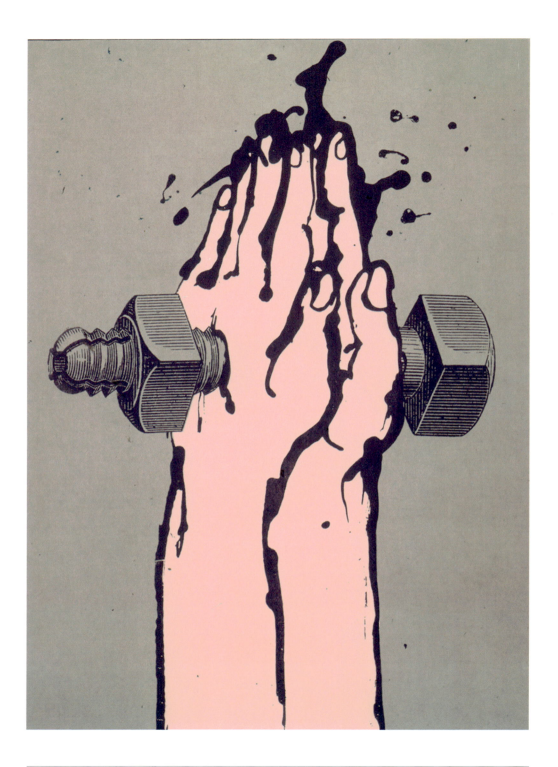

Designer
Lanny Sommese

Country
U.S.A.

Year
1982

50

Designer
Lanny Sommese

Country
U.S.A.

Year
1988

51

Designer
Masuteru Aoba

Country
Japan

Year
1987

Designer
Guillaume Lanneau

Country
France

Year
2010

53

Designer
Svetlana Faldina
Alexander Faldin

Country
Russia

Year
2004

Designer
Fang Chen

Country
China

Year
1998

55

| **Designer** | **Country** | **Year** | 58 |
| Rico Lins | Brazil | 1989 | |

Designer
Rico Lins

Country
Brazil

Year
1996

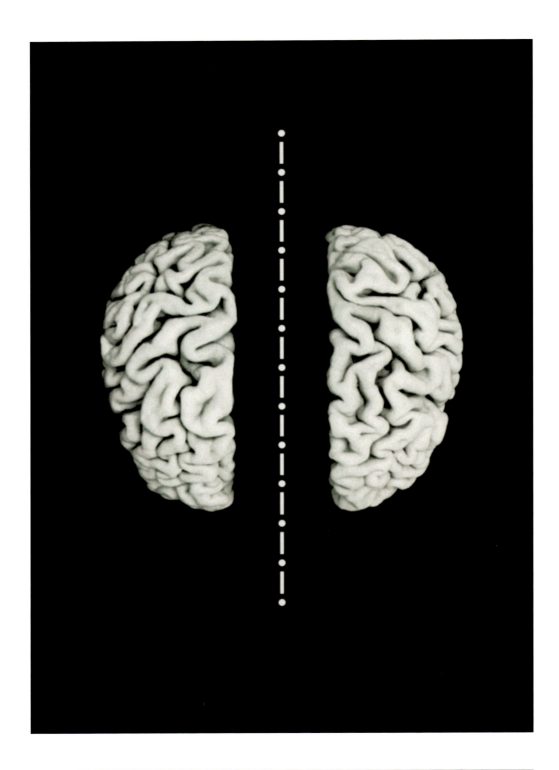

Designer
Svetlana Faldina
Alexander Faldin

Country
Russia

Year
2009

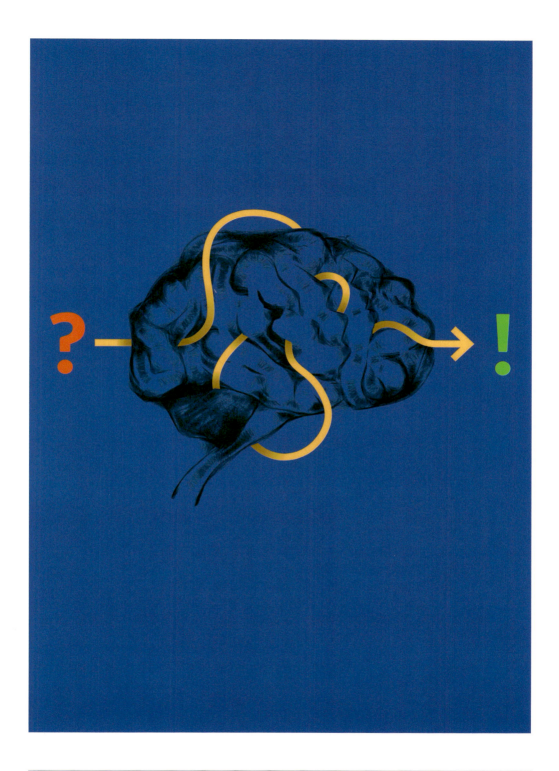

Designer
Ken Carbone

Country
U.S.A.

Year
2010

Designer
Mehmet Ali Türkmen

Country
Turkey

Year
2007

62

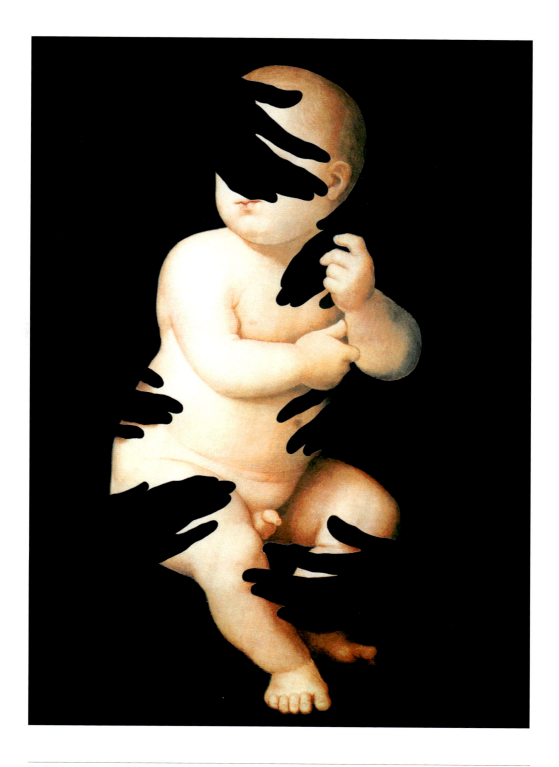

Designer
Alain Le Quernec

Country
France

Year
2008

63

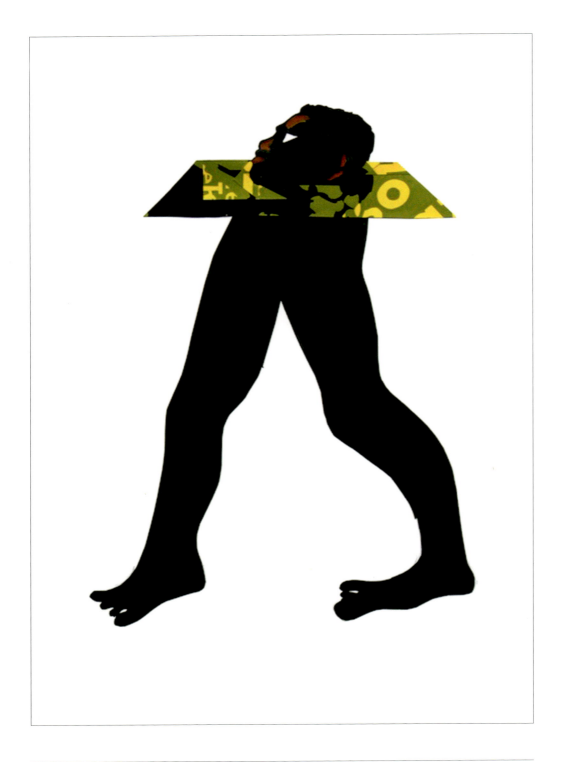

Designer
Franco Balan

Country
Italy

Year
2008

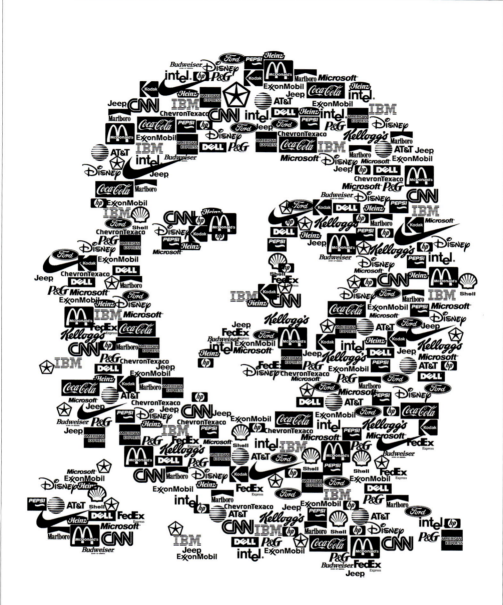

Designer
Patrick Thomas

Country
U.K.

Year
2001

Designer
Mirko Ilić

Country
U.S.A.

Year
2003

Designer
Monika Zawadzki

Country
Poland

Year
2008

Designer
James Cross

Country
U.S.A.

Year
1986

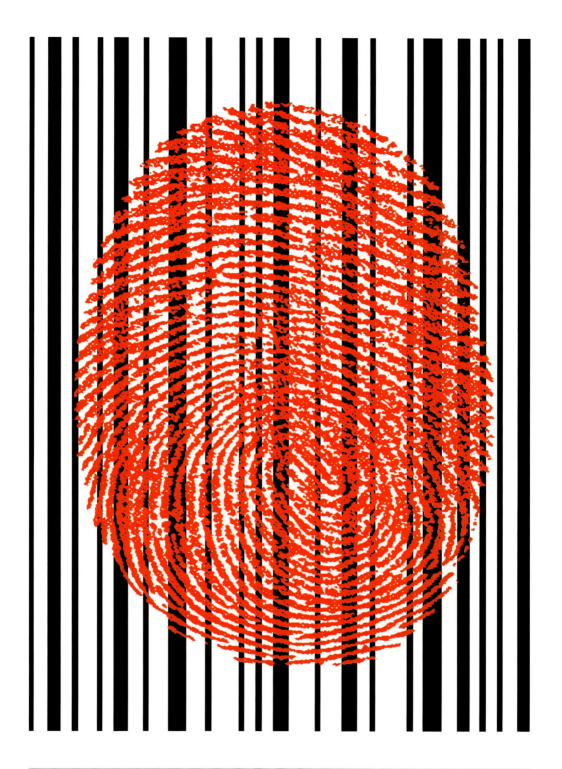

Designer **Designer**
Armando Milani

Country **Country**
Italy

Year **Year**
2008

69

Designer
Shigeo Fukuda

Country
Japan

Year
1989

70

Designer
Shigeo Fukuda

Country
Japan

Year
1992

Designer
Anthon Beeke

Country
The Netherlands

Year
2003

Designer
Monika Zawadzki

Country
Poland

Year
2008

Designer
Sadik Karamustafa

Country
Turkey

Year
1997

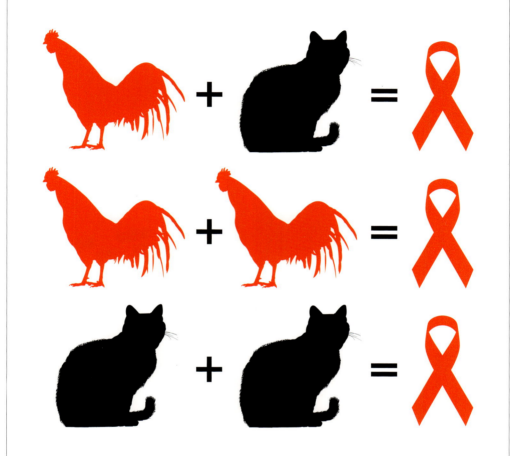

Designer
Garth Walker

Country
South Africa

Year
2008

Designer
Alexander Jordan

Country
France

Year
1991

76

Designer
Nous Travaillons Ensemble
Sébastien Courtois
Valérie Debure
Alex Jordan

Country
France

Year
2011

Designer
Emanuele Luzzati

Country
Italy

Year
1977

Designer
Emanuele Luzzati

Country
Italy

Year
1975

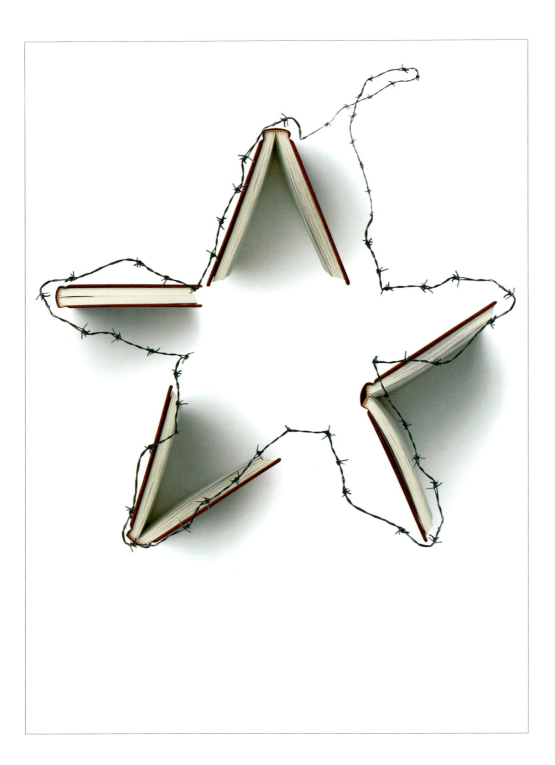

Designer
David Wang Xingong

Country
Taiwan

Year
2008

Designer
Albe Steiner

Country
Italy

Year
1973

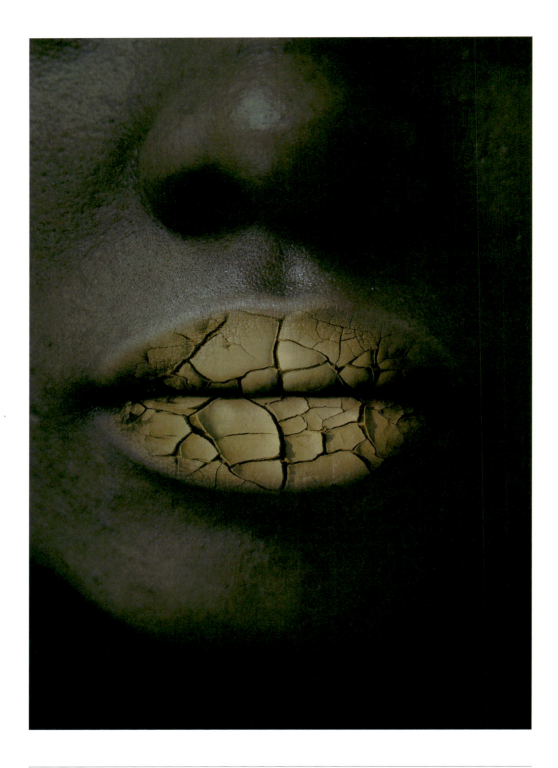

| **Designer** | **Country** | **Year** | 82 |
| Ezio Burani | Italy | 2007 | |

Designer
Katsumi Asaba

Country
Japan

Year
2005

Designer
Patrick Thomas

Country
U.K.

Year
2002

84

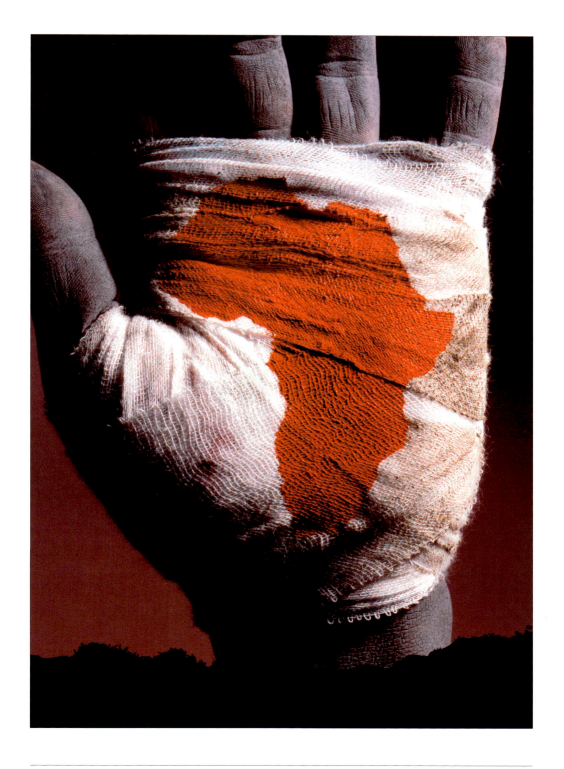

Designer
Gunter Rambow

Country
Germany

Year
1988

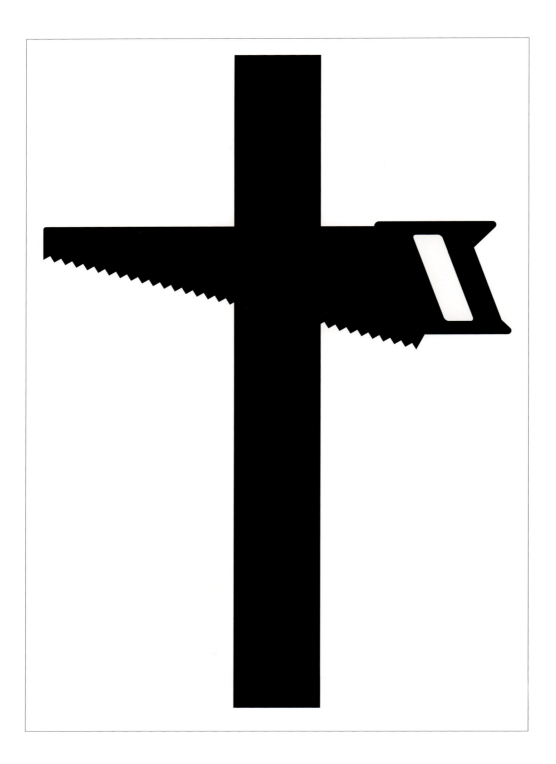

Designer
Herman Van Bostelen

Country
The Netherlands

Year
2009

Designer
Stephan Bundi

Country
Switzerland

Year
1996

Designer
Yossi Lemel

Country
Israel

Year
2012

88

Designer
Yossi Lemel

Country
Israel

Year
2012

89

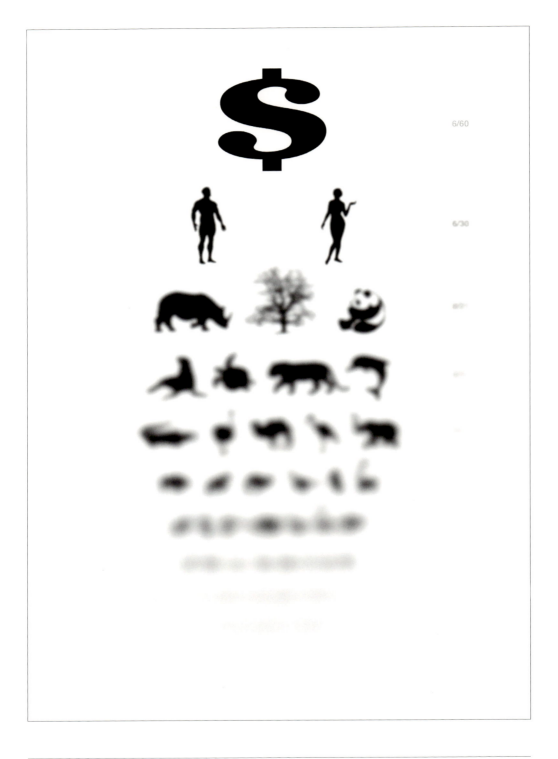

Designer
Fang Chen

Country
China

Year
2010

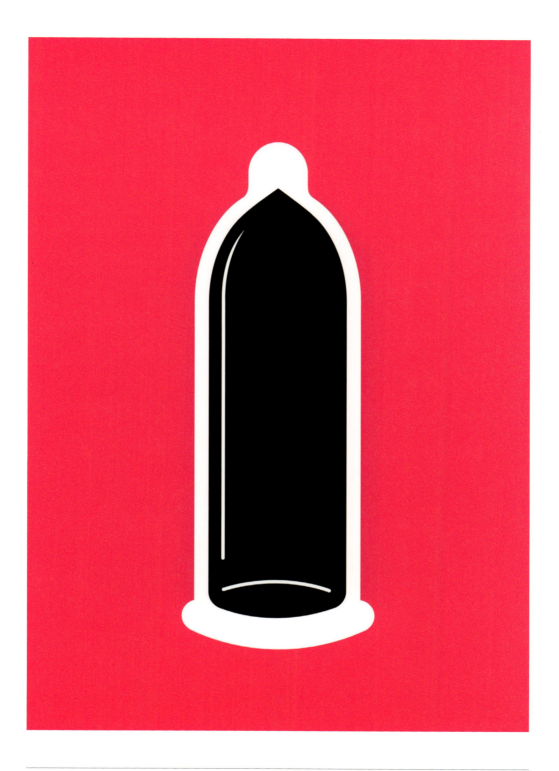

Designer
Fang Chen

Country
China

Year
2010

91

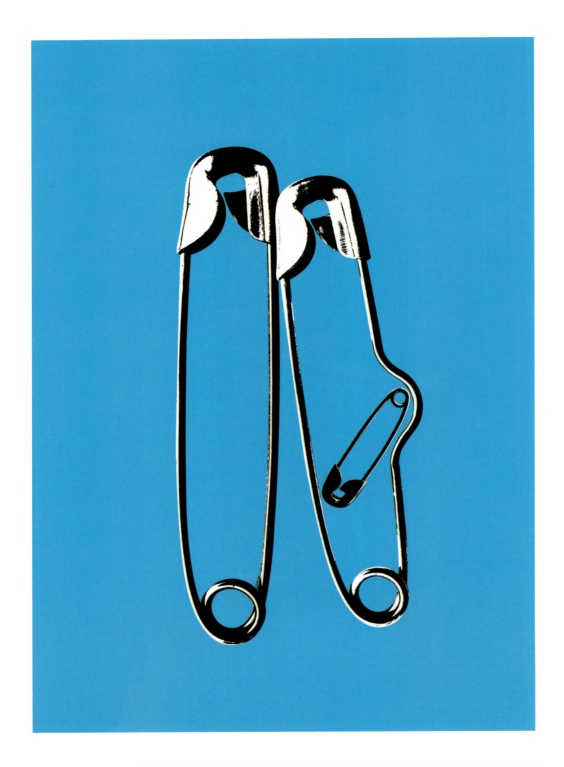

Designer
Parisa Tashakori

Country
Iran

Year
2008

Designer
Parisa Tashakori

Country
Iran

Year
2002

93

Designer
Lex Drewinski

Country
Germany

Year
2012

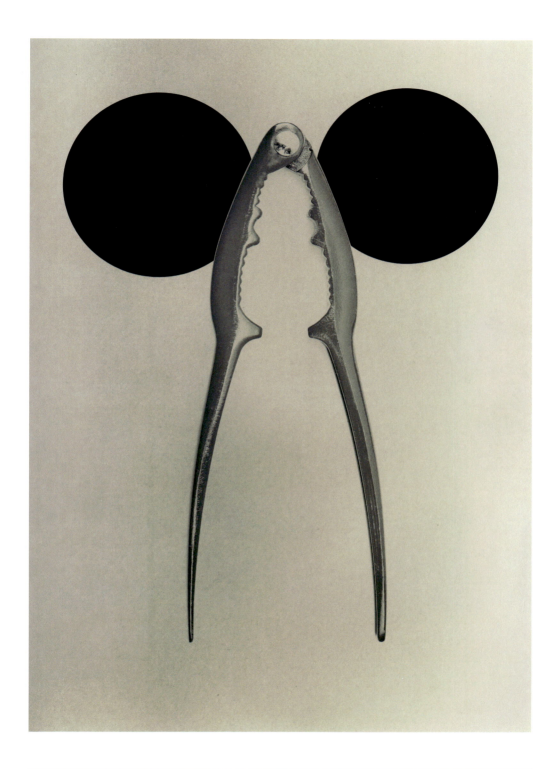

Designer
Robert Appleton

Country
Canada

Year
2010

Designer
Henrik Kubel

Country
U.K.

Year
2010

Designer
Luba Lukova

Country
U.S.A.

Year
1994

Designer
Niklaus Troxler

Country
Switzerland

Year
1992

99

Designer
Leo Lin

Country
Taiwan

Year
2009

Designer
Tapani Aartomaa

Country
Finland

Year
1971

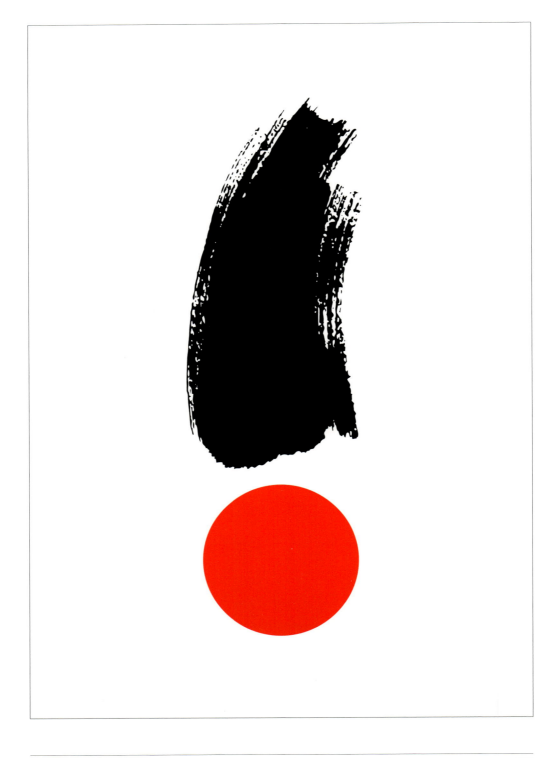

Designer
Raban Ruddigkeit

Country
Germany

Year
2011

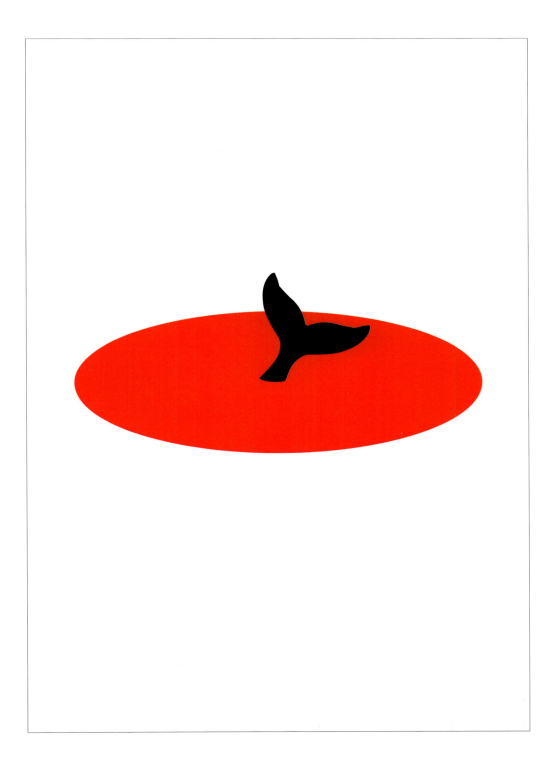

Designer
Lex Drewinski

Country
Germany

Year
2008

Designer
U.G. Sato

Country
Japan

Year
1993

106

Designer
U.G. Sato

Country
Japan

Year
1993

107

Designer
Wojtek KOREK Korkuć

Country
Poland

Year
2006

108

Designer
Isidro Ferrer

Country
Spain

Year
2008

109

Designer
Pekka Loiri

Country
Finland

Year
2009

110

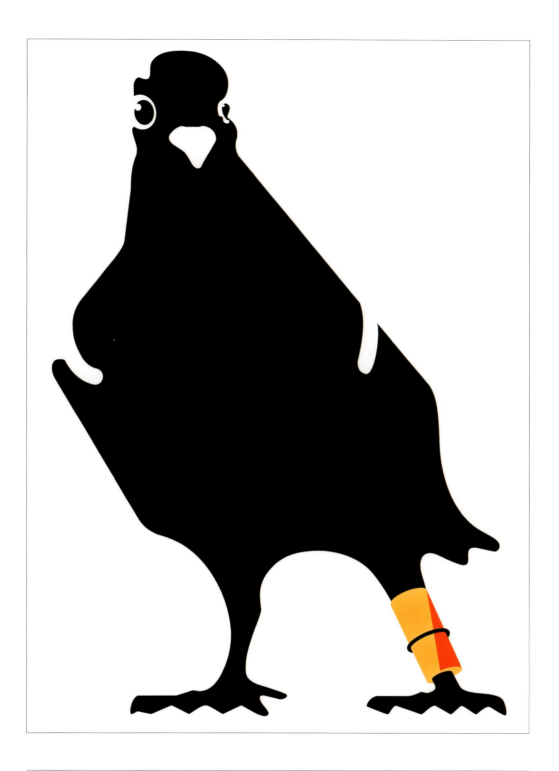

Designer
Pekka Loiri

Country
Finland

Year
2010

111

Designer
Alain Le Quernec

Country
France

Year
2008

Designer
Marlena Buczek

Country
U.S.A.

Year
2010

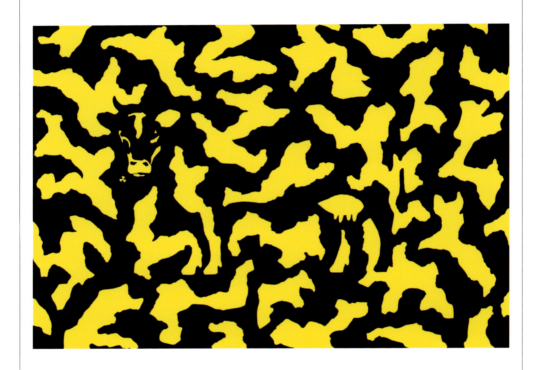

Designer
Uwe Loesch

Country
Germany

Year
1986

Designer
Uwe Loesch

Country
Germany

Year
1985

Designer
Marlena Buczek

Country
U.S.A.

Year
2009

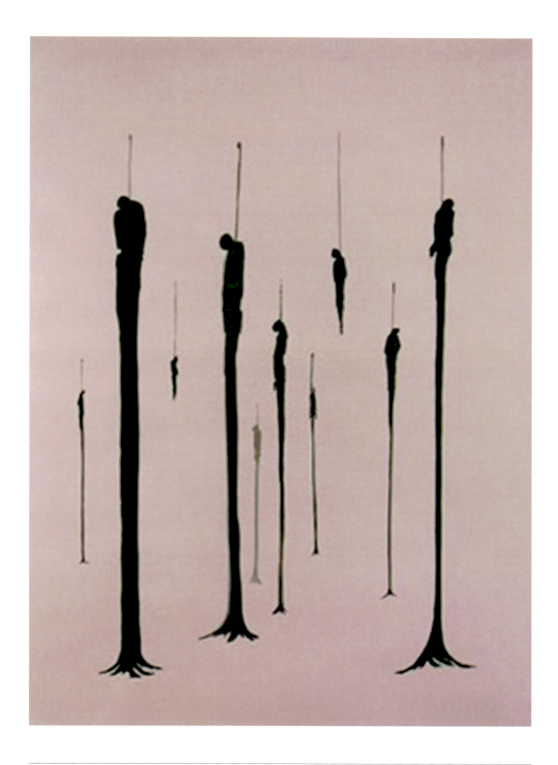

Designer
Eli Kince

Country
U.S.A.

Year
1994

117

Designer
Jochen Fiedler

Country
Germany

Year
2002

118

Designer
Yuri Surkov

Country
Russia

Year
1995

119

Designer
Chatri na Ranong

Country
Australia

Year
2007

120

Designer
Mirko Ilić

Country
U.S.A.

Year
2009

Designer
Mirko Ilić

Country
U.S.A.

Year
1996

122

Designer
Unknown

Country
Czech Republic

Year
1975

123

Designer
Alexander Faldin

Country
Russia

Year
1985

124

Designer
Pierre Mendell

Country
Germany

Year
1993

125

Designer
Kyösti Varis

Country
Finland

Year
1971

126

Designer
Kyösti Varis

Country
Finland

Year
1971

127

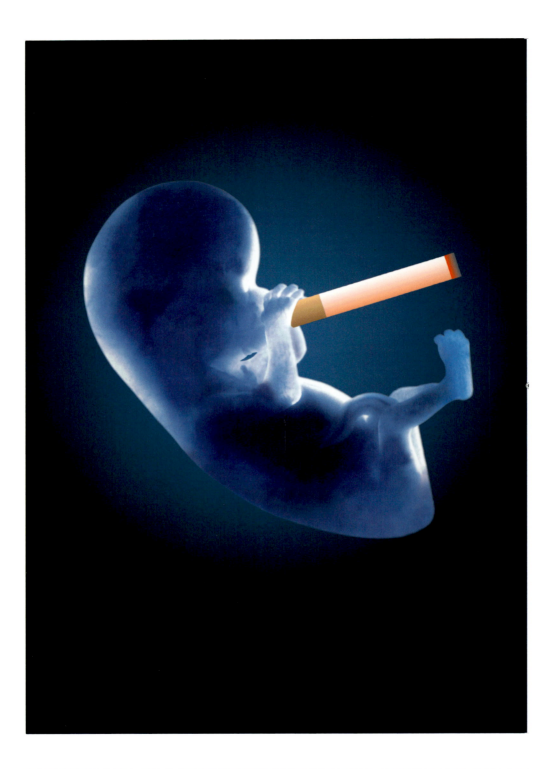

Designer
Alain Le Quernec

Country
France

Year
2003

128

Designer
Armando Milani

Country
Italy

Year
2003

Designer
Kyösti Varis

Country
Finland

Year
2002

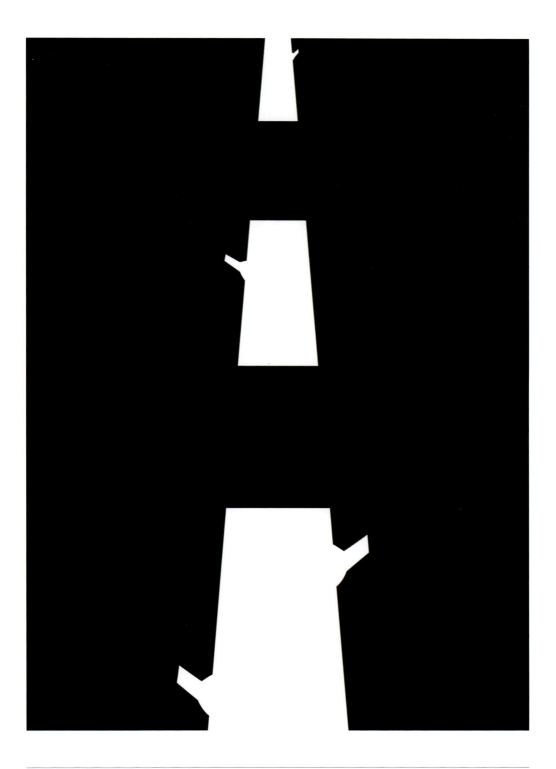

Designer
Lex Drewinski

Country
Germany

Year
2008

Designer
Momayez Morteza

Country
Iran

Year
1976

132

Designer
Momayez Morteza

Country
Iran

Year
1978

Designer
Gunter Rambow

Country
Germany

Year
1979

Designer
Gunter Rambow

Country
Germany

Year
1979

135

Designer
Patrick Thomas

Country
U.K.

Year
2007

136

Designer
Patrick Thomas

Country
U.K.

Year
2001

137

Designer
Hilppa Hyrkäs

Country
Finland

Year
1994

138

Designer
Niklaus Troxler

Country
Switzerland

Year
1996

139

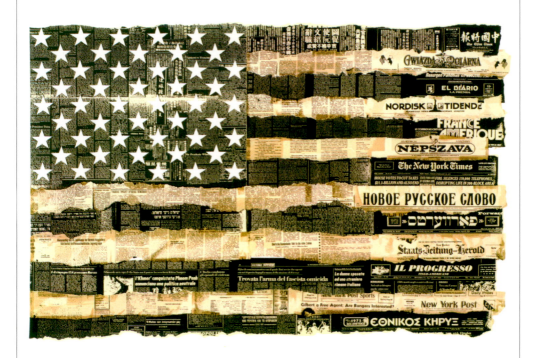

Designer
Massimo Vignelli

Country
U.S.A.

Year
1976

Designer
Louis Danziger

Country
U.S.A.

Year
1965

141

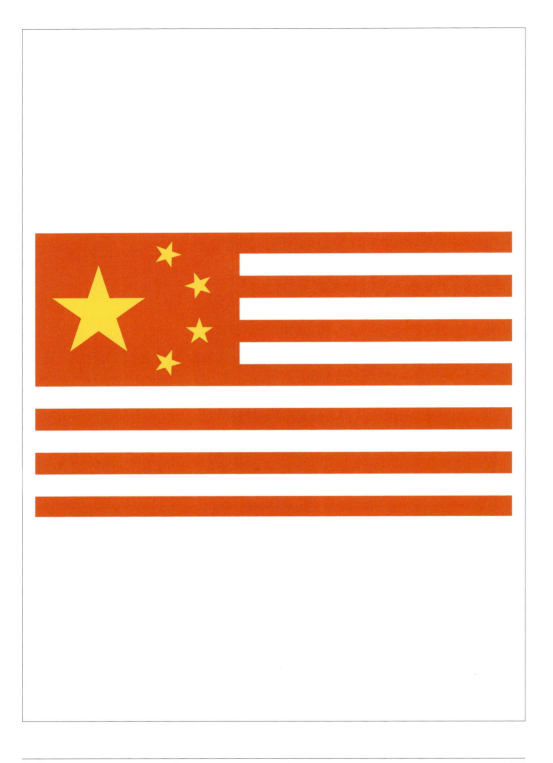

Designer
Woody Pirtle

Country
U.S.A.

Year
2012

Designer
Bob Gill

Country
U.S.A.

Year
1970

143

Designer
Maurizio Milani

Country
Italy

Year
2000

144

Designer
Wojtek KOREK Korkuć

Country
Poland

Year
2010

145

Designer
Isidro Ferrer

Country
Spain

Year
2009

Designer
Pierre Mendell

Country
Germany

Year
1998

147

Designer
Ivan Chermayeff

Country
U.S.A.

Year
1999

148

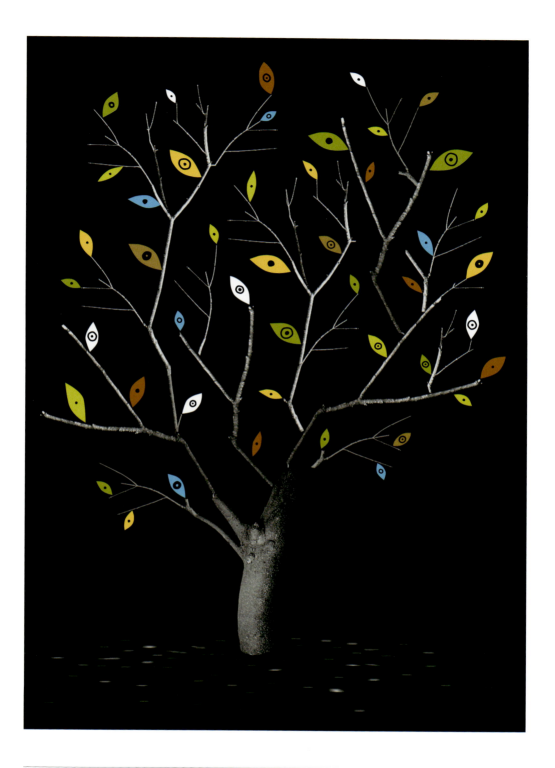

Designer
Michael Mabry

Country
U.S.A.

Year
2000

149

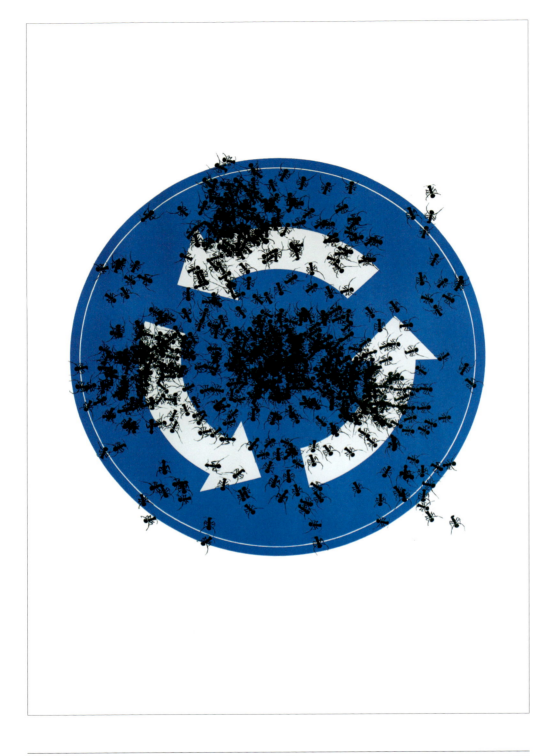

Designer
Pino Tovaglia

Country
Italy

Year
1967

Designer
Fabrice Praeger

Country
France

Year
2012

151

Designer
Germán Montalvo

Country
Mexico

Year
1992

152

Designer
Germán Montalvo

Country
Mexico

Year
1990

153

Designer
Melchior Imboden

Country
Switzerland

Year
2006

154

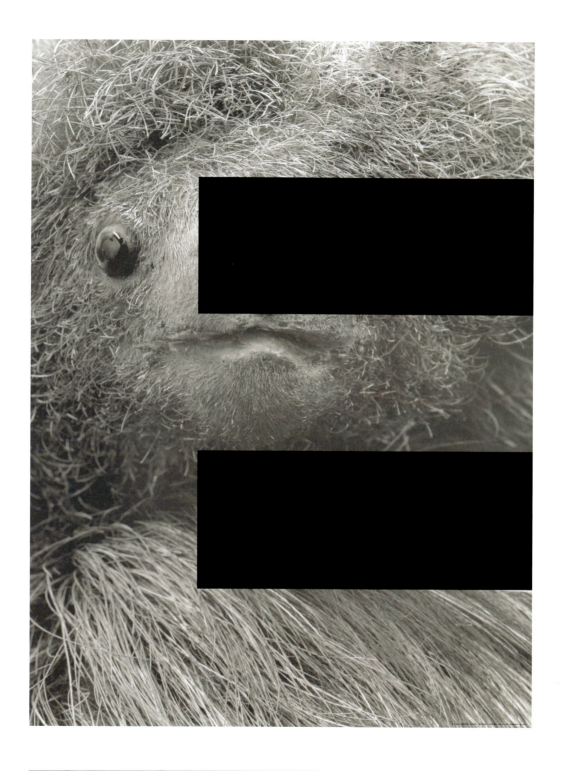

Designer
Melchior Imboden

Country
Switzerland

Year
2006

Designer
Bruno Munari

Country
Italy

Year
1972

156

Designer
Bruno Munari

Country
Italy

Year
1970

Designer
James Cross

Country
U.S.A.

Year
1991

Designer
James Cross

Country
U.S.A.

Year
1991

159

Designer
Giulio Confalonieri

Country
Italy

Year
1966

Designer
Giulio Confalonieri

Country
Italy

Year
1970

161

Designer
George Tscherny

Country
U.S.A.

Year
2013

163

Designer
Paul Rand

Country
U.S.A.

Year
1982

164

Designer
James Cross

Country
U.S.A.

Year
1978

Designer
Bob Gill

Country
U.S.A.

Year
1965

166

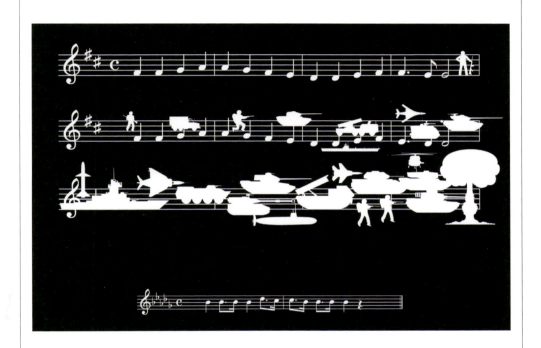

Designer
Svetlana Faldina
Alexander Faldin

Country
Russia

Year
1994

Designer
Milton Glaser

Country
U.S.A.

Year
1968

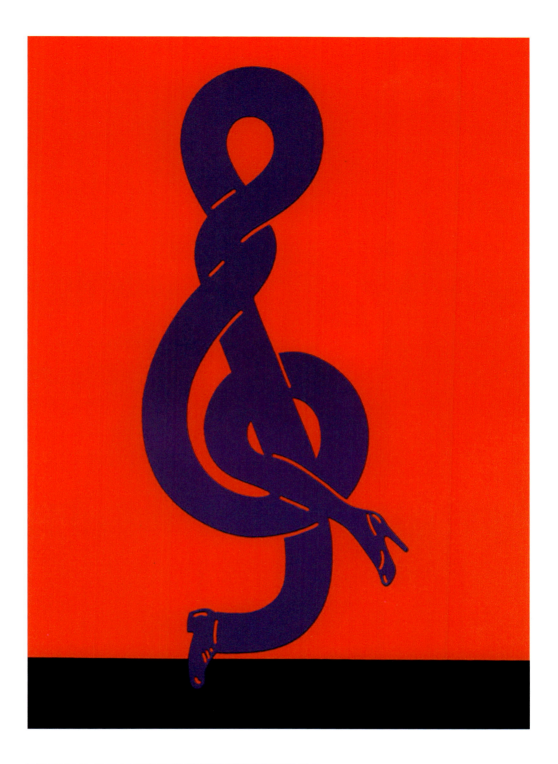

Designer
Shigeo Fukuda

Country
Japan

Year
1988

169

Designer
Armin Hofmann

Country
Switzerland

Year
1993

170

Designer
Armin Hofmann

Country
Switzerland

Year
1993

Designer
Bruno Oldani

Country
Norway

Year
1987

172

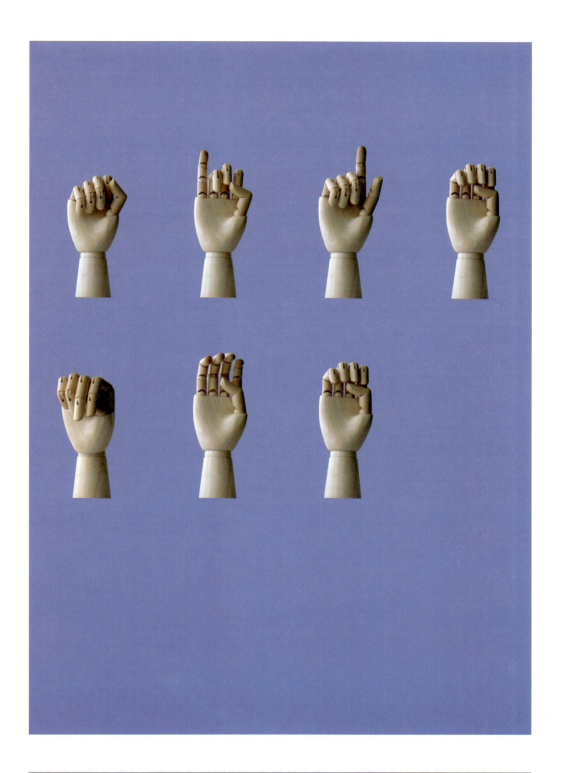

Designer
Arnold Schwartzman

Country
U.S.A.

Year
2012

Designer
Bruno Monguzzi

Country
Switzerland

Year
2011

174

Designer
Bruno Monguzzi

Country
Switzerland

Year
2001

175

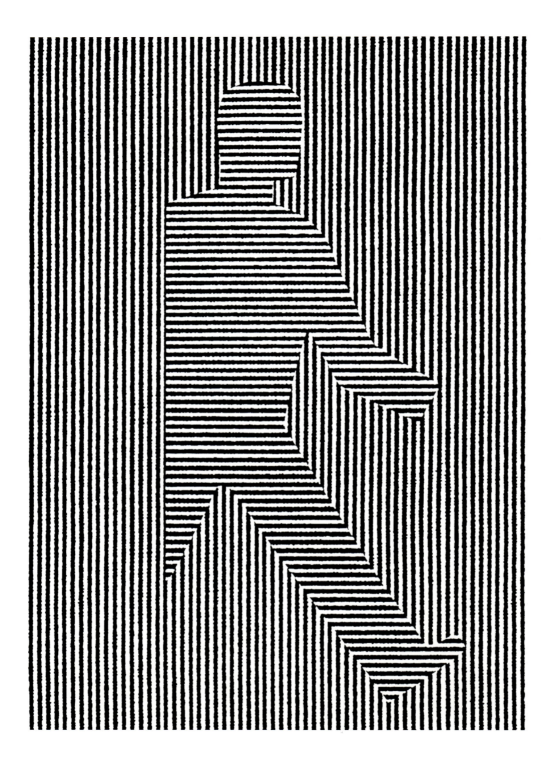

Designer
Gérard Paris-Clavel

Country
France

Year
2001

176

Designer
Roman Cieslewicz

Country
Poland

Year
1964

177

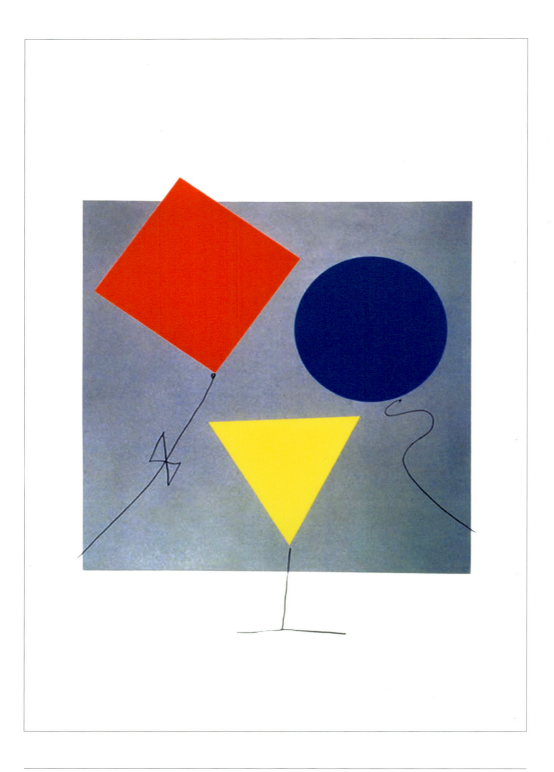

Designer
Alan Fletcher

Country
U.K.

Year
1982

178

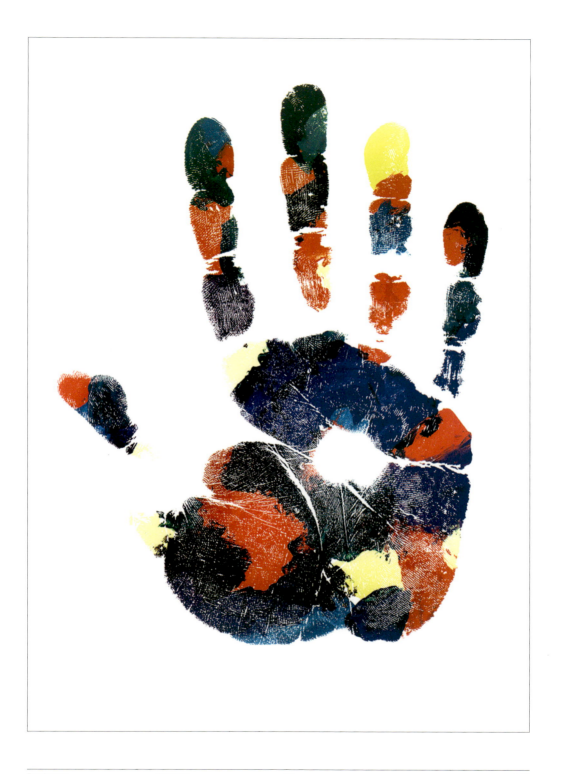

Designer
Alan Fletcher

Country
U.K.

Year
1993

179

Designer
Wojtek KOREK Korkuć

Country
Poland

Year
2001

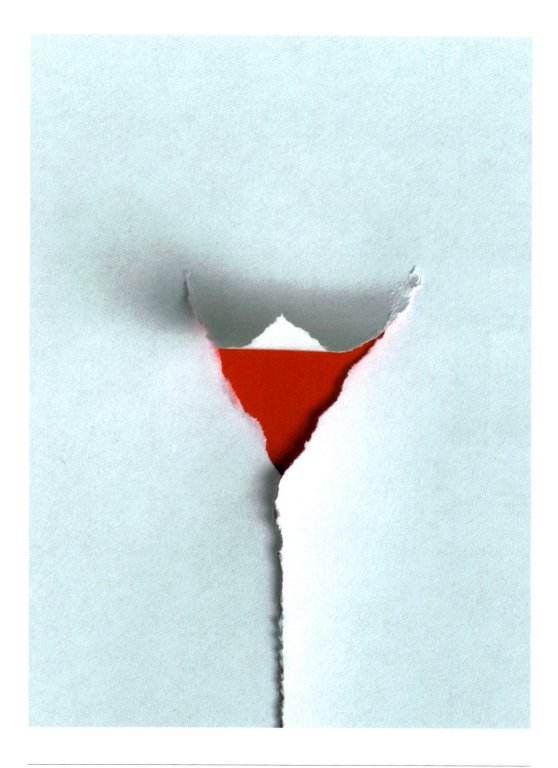

Designer
Pierre Mendell

Country
Germany

Year
1998

181

Designer
Armando Milani

Country
Italy

Year
2008

182

Designer
Ivan Chermayeff

Country
U.S.A.

Year
1983

183

Designer
Patrick Thomas

Country
U.K.

Year
2007

Designer
Fritz Gottschalk

Country
Switzerland

Year
1965

185

Designer
Ikko Tanaka

Country
Japan

Year
1958

186

Designer
Ikko Tanaka

Country
Japan

Year
1972

187

Designer
Leszek Zebrowski

Country
Poland

Year
2009

188

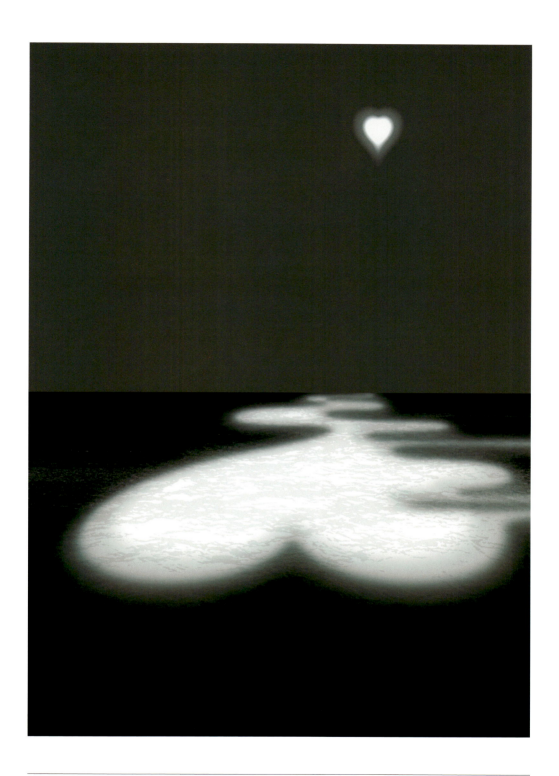

Designer
Yano Kashimi

Country
Japan

Year
2010

189

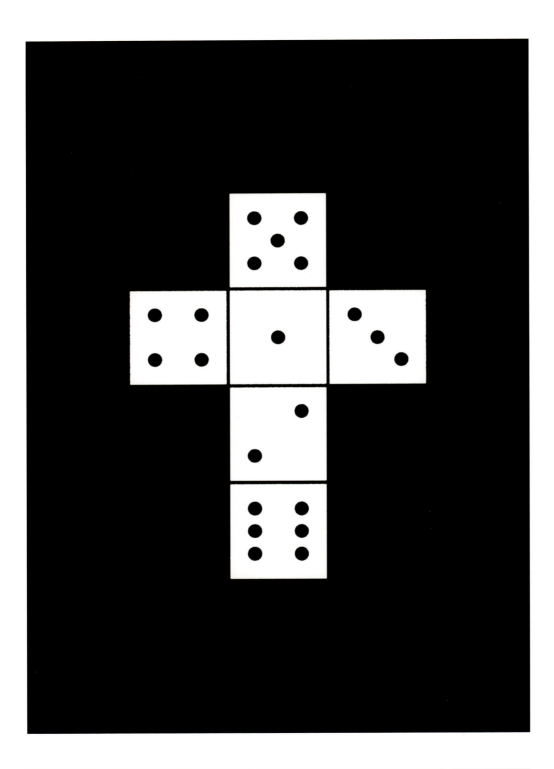

Designer
Stefano Asili

Country
Italy

Year
1987

Designer
Chaz Maviyane-Davies
Paul Peter Piech

Country
Zimbabwe
U.S.A.

Year
1980

191

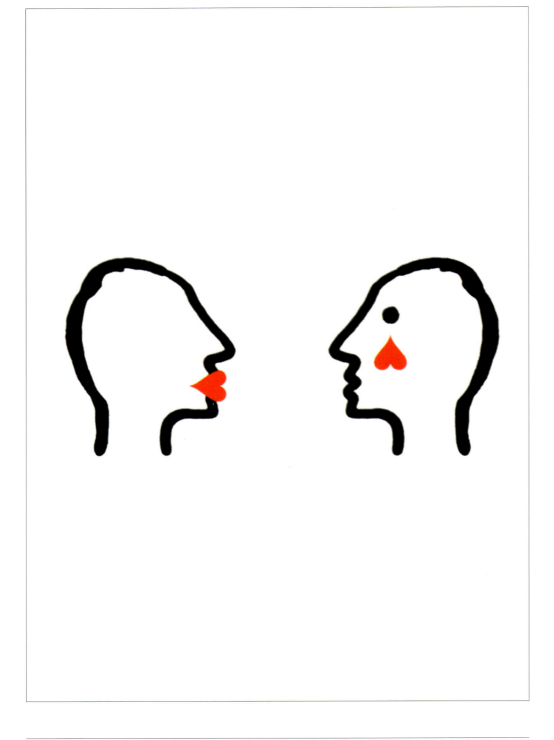

Designer
Fabrice Praeger

Country
France

Year
1996

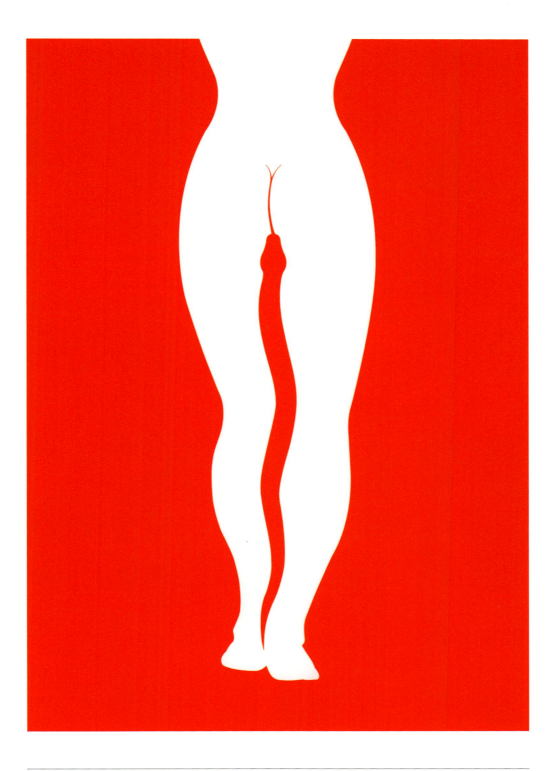

Designer
Lex Drewinski

Country
Germany

Year
1996

193

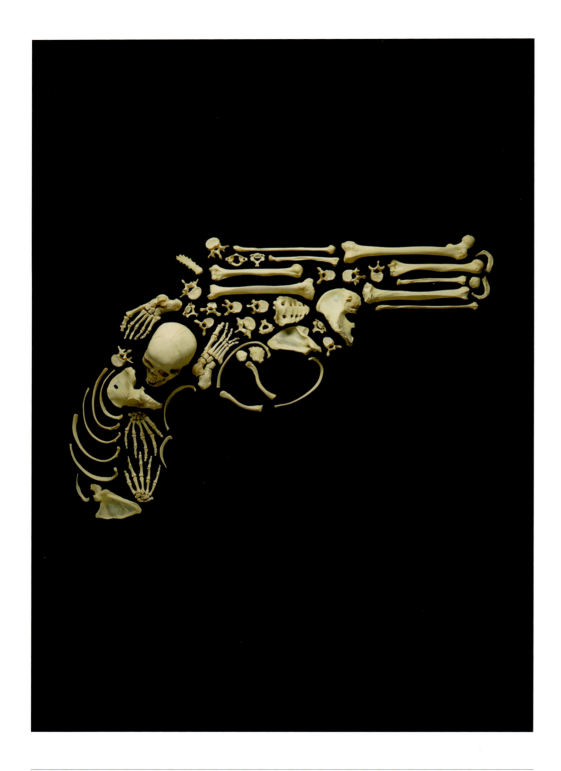

Designer
François Robert

Country
U.S.A.

Year
2007

194

Designer
Massimo Dolcini

Country
Italy

Year
1980

195

Original posters and descriptions

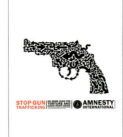

Cover
Armando Milani

An eye for an eye
makes the whole
world blind.
Mahatma Gandhi

Page 6
Woody Pirtle

This poster was created to
support an initiative by Amnesty
International to stop the
trafficking of arms that could
contribute to serious human
rights violations, crimes against
humanity, or war crimes.

Page 7
Stefan Sagmeister
Matthias Ernstberger

This poster was part of a series
of punctuation symbols, where
each symbol was celebrated on
a poster designed by a different
designer.
We wound up with the
apostrophe, whose job it is to
eliminate a letter.
Hence the warm gun...

Page 8
Albe Steiner

Peace.
Poster winner of the Peace
International Competition
in Vienna, 1956.

Page 9
Luba Lukova

Peace.
The poster addresses the
duality of war and peace. If you
wish for peace, prepare for war,
that's the old saw. But can we
really protect peace by creating
more wars?

Page 10
Masuteru Aoba

Peace.

Page 11
Steff Geissbühler

Peace.

Page 12
Shigeo Fukuda

Next Victory.
Poster against the war.

Page 13
Chaz Maviyane-Davies

World AIDS Day.
AIDS awareness.
For Centre of Design of
Rosario, Argentina.

Page 14
Ivan Chermayeff

"War and Peace" (a television
production of Tolstoy produced
by Mobil Oil).

Page 15
Ivan Chermayeff

Peace.
For the Shoshin Society,
remembering the 40th
anniversary of the bombing at
Hiroshima.

Page 16
Yossi Lemel

WarPeace.
The sea of soldiers surrounding
the dove of peace. They threa-
ten to sweep it as a symbol of
the waves of violence and the
ritual of war in our society.
This is reality; on the other hand
there is the dream of peace.

Page 17
Yossi Lemel

PeaceWar.
In a utopian world when waves
of doves of peace will win
"The War." This is the situation
the biblical prophets wished for.
The soldier raising his hand was
built by me especially for this
poster.

Page 18
U.G. Sato

Peace.
Flying to peace.

Page 19
U.G. Sato

Mt. Fuji.
The famous Mt. Fuji in Japan is
the symbol of peace.

Page 20
Yoshiro Kamekura

Hiroshima appeals.

Page 21
Federica Marangoni

Light is always free.
An LED red butterfly beating in
a cage, a symbolic shape for
life. Light escapes from the bars
of a strong iron cage where the
butterfly is imprisoned.

Page 22
Isidro Ferrer

Protesting Spain's participation
in the invasion of Iraq in 2003.
Responding to a phrase from
George W. Bush: "The invasion
of Iraq was a preventive war."
The toothbrush also prevents
cavities, but this brush of nails
goes beyond preventive hygiene.

Page 23
Armando Milani

Constantly risking death.
Poster for the Ferlinghetti book,
50 Poems and 50 Posters.
When mistreated, weak people
can become very dangerous.

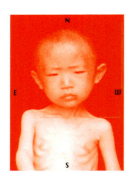

Page 24
Uwe Loesch

NEWS North-Korea 2001.

Page 25
B. Martin Pedersen

Lisa with hurt doll.
Photographer:
Armen Kachaturian.

Page 26
Chaz Maviyane-Davies

No More Hunger.
Poster for an exhibition on
stopping world hunger.
For Centre of Design Rosario,
Argentina.

Page 27
Jukka Veistola

Prize in International/Global
Poster Competition of UNICEF
in Paris 1969.
This poster is one of the four
Finnish Posters in the Collection
in the Museum of Modern Art
in New York.

Page 28
Jukka Veistola

Prize in Nordic Peace Poster
Competition in Copenhagen,
1970. Third prize in International
Poster Biennale in Brno, 1972.

Page 29
Maciej Urbaniec

"ABC," from collection of
Krzysztof Dydo.
Krakow, Poland.

Page 30
Uwe Loesch

Poster against armament in the
Western and Eastern World
during the Cold War.
Client: Le Mouvement de la
Paix, Paris.

Page 31
Grapus

Vietnam. A people united
and determined to win their
independence.
Series 1.

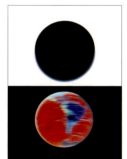

Page 32
Grapus

Vietnam. A people united
and determined to win their
independence.
Series 2.

Page 33
Grapus

Vietnam. A people united
and determined to win their
independence.
Series 3.

Page 34
Werner Jeker

Human rights declaration.
Campaign poster.

Page 35
Werner Jeker

Cambio de Milenio.
Campaign poster for the Millen-
nium (Chile).

Page 36
Isidro Ferrer

Cartel para la obra de teatro
"Un enemigo del pueblo"
de Henrik Ibsen.

Page 37
2xGoldstein
Constructive Modifier

Human action should always be
constructive, never destructive.
Deliberative action is the way.
The Constructive Modifier
is an image for transformation
from aggression into inspiration.

Page 38
John Rushworth

The poster had to be
all-inclusive and evoke a strong
emotional response worldwide.
The competition was open to
all members of the Alliance
Graphique Internationale and
potential members endorsed
or recommended by the elite
graphics organisation.
Pentagram partner John
Rushworth, an AGI member,
produced a poster which
"eliminated" images of
violence with a graphic pun.

Page 39
Koichi Sato

Image for the International
Design Center in Nagoya.
The opening announcement
of a designers' firm IdcN,
representing the moment when
one touches the new thing after
probing in the dark.
It is my five fingertips touching
the glass on a photocopier.

Page 40
Kari Piippo

Lahti Poster Museum
Anniversary Poster.

Page 41
Stephan Bundi

Stop torture.
A poster for Amnesty
International that was exhibited
at MoMA (NY) in 1990. First
Prize at the International Poster
Trienniale in Mons, Belgium.

Page 42
Fons Hickmann

When eyes could still speak.
For Silent Movie Festival Graz.
The emergence of film is rooted
in an attempt to capture life and
take it deeper into newfound
realms of beauty and horror.
The history of film is largely
shaped by a drive for perfection,
and yet the charm of film
springs partly from mistakes
and perfection.

Page 43
Chatri na Ranong

We all bleed the same colour.
Good 50 x 70.

Page 44
Sergio Olivotti

The Egg, an archetypal symbol of life and birth, develops weapons of defense towards an unknown enemy.
The poster has clear political roots, but it aims to be a universal admonition against prejudicially hostile attitudes.

Page 45
Woody Pirtle

Abuse of Power.
This piece was created for a show of images interpreting various writings on the abuse of power. Curated by the multi-disciplinary design firm, Collins.

Page 46
Jianping He

Chinese fashion, chinese culture. 99 Ningbo & culture poster exhibition.

Page 47
Jianping He

Leid-KultuR.

Page 48
Milton Glaser

We are all Africans.
A social awarness campaign, to bring recognition of our solidarity with African people today.

Page 49
Armando Milani

Man's fight for freedom.
Series of movies for Cineclub Brera, Milan.

Page 50
Lanny Sommese

Two hands bolted together. Concept: the idea was to depict mans inhumanity to man/ torture, which hopefully would heighten public awareness of the issue and, in turn, explain why the Amnesty organization is around. The visceral drip drawing style of the praying hands was used to contrast the mechanically drawn bolt and heighten the emotional impact of image. The bolt and hands were scaled and juxtaposed to appear as a cross, which added to the meaning and made the image more emblematic.

Page 51
Lanny Sommese

Silhouetted is a chain link fence with hands touching. Concept: HOPE. Unlike my other Amnesty posters, the idea here is not to depict the human torment that Amnesty is trying to alleviate, but rather to focus on the positive aspects of the work of Amnesty International. Helping hands are weakening or breaking down the fences of tyranny etc. — offering a glow of hope and/or giving aid to those in need. Michelangelo's painting The Creation of Adam on the Sistine Ceiling played a big part in this poster conceptually.

Page 52
Masuteru Aoba

Are you dumping the earth?

Page 53
Guillaume Lanneau

L'Internationale sera le genre humain.

Page 54
Svetlana Faldina
Alexander Faldin

Crime/punishment. Against sexual violence.

Page 55
Fang Chen

The hand is intended to symbolize all of humankind. I felt the capitalized "V" represented by the two fingers is a universal symbol for victory and understood by viewers of all races and cultures.

Page 56
Wojtec KOREK Korkuć

Tango.
Theater poster.

Page 57
Alexandra Faldina
Anastasia Faldina

Social inequality.

Page 58
Rico Lins

During the bicentennial commemorations of the French Revolution, an international group of 66 designers was invited to create a poster alluding to the Declaration of Human Rights, and to participate in an international forum on the social role of graphic design. The posters produced resulted in an exhibition in Paris, followed by simultaneous launches in various cities worldwide.

Page 59
Rico Lins

Poster for an international congress on graphic design that gathered Brazilian and American designers affiliated with the AGI– Alliance Graphique Internationale. Rico Lins was in charge of the creative direction for the event, as well as the whole communications campaign.

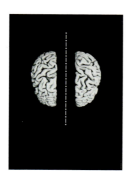

Page 60
Svetlana Faldina
Alexander Faldin

Berlin Wall.

Page 61
Ken Carbone

Poster design for the 2010 AGI
Congress/Porto.
The theme was creative
processes in graphic design.

Page 62
Mehmet Ali Türkmen

Hafriyat Art Group's invitational
poster exhibition: "Sense of
Fear" throughout the history
of mankind. Fear of God and
conscience.

Page 63
Alain Le Quernec

About pedophily.
Some years before I was
working on a poster about the
sudden death of the newborn
child. The idea was to take off
the child from a renaissance
nativity painting.
When I did it, I noticed that
the baby shape was cut away
where the mother's hands had
been. I remembered this disturbing effect and magnified it
when I was asked to make this
antipedophily message.

Page 64
Franco Balan

Human Rights Violations.

Page 65
Patrick Thomas

Che.

Page 66
Mirko Ilić

Last Taboo.
This image is about interracial
relationships as the last taboo
in the US.

Page 67
Monika Zawadzki

A Journey Round the Skull.
Exhibition poster, Centre for
Contemporary Art in Warsaw.
Boundless and unpredictable
human mind.

Page 68
James Cross

Interpretation of the theme
Connections.
For Simpson Paper Company.

Page 69
Armando Milani

I am not a number.
Each one has his own identity.
For Wolfsonian Museum Miami.

Page 70
Shigeo Fukuda

Human Rights.

Page 71
Shigeo Fukuda

Rio 92. United Nations
Conference on enviroment and
development.

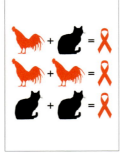

Page 72
Anthon Beeke

Design Academy Eindhoven.
The White Lady.

Page 73
Monika Zawadzki

Women's Rights. From the
series "Human and Animal
Rights".

Page 74
Sadik Karamustafa

Contribution to the poster
project curated by David
Tartakover "Sharing Jerusalem /
Two Capitals for Two States."

Page 75
Garth Walker

Cock & Pussy = AIDS, icon.
Saint-Etienne International
Design, Biennale, France.

Page 76
Alexander Jordan

Image for a Grapus / Nous
Travaillons Ensemble exhibition
about the US - Mexican border.

Page 77
Nous Travaillons Ensemble

Sébastien Courtois
Valérie Debure
Alex Jordan
A memory trail for migrations.
Grand Prix / Lahti Poster
Biennial, Finland.

Page 78
Emanuele Luzzati

Gazza e Charlot
(Magpie and Charlot).
Sketch for poster of the film
festival, mixed media and
collage.

Page 79
Emanuele Luzzati

Il Visconte Dimezzato
(The Cloven Viscount).
Sketch for Calvino's book,
mixed media and collage.

Page 80
David Wang Xingong

My reading image.
The poster delivers the reading
experience in my youth
memory which was under the
shadow of the martial law.

Page 81
Albe Steiner

For political and racial
extermination in the Nazis'
camps.
Museum Monument Carpi.

Page 82
Ezio Burani

How to create a powerful
poster without words? The
idea was to join together two
images already known in
several social campaigns:
a dry land and a black person,
but to create a link between
the territory and the inhabitants
launching the message: my lips
are dry like my land.

Page 83
Katsumi Asaba

This is a graphic design simply
showing a glass of water.
On the left there is one drop
of water.
This is a new way of expressing
the Kanji character.
I believe inventing future
symbols is one of the important
works of design.

Page 84
Patrick Thomas

Africa.

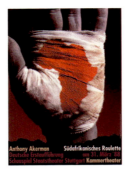

Page 85
Gunter Rambow

Suedafrikanisches Roulette.
Even today, Africa is still
bleeding.
The poster from 1988 shows
a bandaged hand with African
blood stain. It was made for
a theatre play called South
African Roulette.

Page 86
Herman Van Bostelen

Addressing the sexual abuse
accusations against the
Catholic Church.

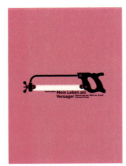

Page 87
Stephan Bundi

Mein Leben als Versager.
Poster advertising a
book, Stories About a Worker
that fails.
Wordplay: "Versager" means
both "failure" and "saw".

Page 88
Yossi Lemel

Low Battery.
Exploiting and squeezing earth's
resources will eventually leave
us all empty.
Using the cellular battery
metaphor, which is recognized
everywhere today, is a warning
sign to stop consuming
unlimitedly, without thinking
about future generations.

Page 89
Yossi Lemel

Carrrrrrt.
Portrays iconic shopping cart,
with a twist - more vicious,
aggressive, and more biting.
The shopping cart with the
teeth symbolizes the greediness,
the endless consumption, the
"biting" capitalism, in its worst
form, that eventually eats your
savings and security in the
endless race. The metaphor
symbolizes a wild beast, a
predator, and the colors (red and
white) symbolize, on the one
hand, blood and bones, and on
the other hand, a very well known
product, Maybe... Coca Cola?

Page 90
Fang Chen

Myopia.
Nowadays many people around
the world are suffering from
myopia, they can't see anything
clearly, (including themselves)
except DOLLAR.

Page 91
Fang Chen

Aid for AIDS.
This poster depicts an image
of a missile or bullet covered by
a tight-fitting condom.
The combination of the two
objects creates an effective
anti-AIDS message.
The stylistic approach
incorporates the optical illusion
created by the interplay of
positive and negative shapes,
either use a condom for safe
sex or be killed by the bullet.

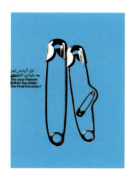

Page 92
Parisa Tashakori

Test your partner before you
make the final decision.
Anti AIDS poster exhibition
in Ukraine.

Page 93
Parisa Tashakori

Create a blue sky for our
children. Iran environment
ministry.

Page 94
Lex Drewinski

This untitled poster has been
created on the topic "we are
99%" of the Occupy Wall
Street movement.
Those 99% stand for the
majority of poor people in
contradiction to the top earning
1%. It generally speaks about
injustice.

Page 95
Pasquale Volpe

For "The Nutcracker", San
Carlo Theatre, Naples.

Page 96
Robert Appleton

For the FIFA World Cup.
The premier international
association football
tournament in South Africa.

Page 97
Henrik Kubel

Kræftens Bekæmpelse /
The Danish Cancer Society.
Commissioned by the Danish
Art Foundation.
500 copies of the poster were
posted across Copenhagen
city during October 2010 – the
international Breast Cancer
Awareness month.

Page 98
Luba Lukova

Ecology.
The poster speaks about the
interdependence of humans
and nature. When we destroy
nature, we destroy ourselves.

Page 99
Niklaus Troxler

Dead Trees.
For the first UN Ecological
Congress in Rio de Janeiro.

Page 100
Leo Lin

Increasing temperature results
in sea level rise.
I am trying to reveal this
environmental issue in my work.
I hope this work will appeal
to everyone to take care of
our environment and love this
planet.

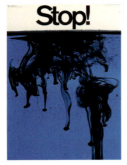

Page 101
Tapani Aartomaa

Stop.
For Protection of Waters.
Photo: Leo Nieminen.

Page 102
Raban Ruddigkeit

A poster (and a bag) to help
the people in Japan after the
nuclear disaster.

Page 103
Lex Drewinski

Stop whaling in Japan.
Ecological poster.

Page 104
Hilppa Hyrkäs

Against global warming, for
Friends of the Earth, Finland.

Page 105
Uwe Loesch

Highnoon. Kyoto Environmental
Poster Design Exhibition.
During the third session of the
conference of the parties to
the UN Convention on Climate
Change.

Page 106
U.G. Sato

Where can Nature go?
These posters were designed
asking for coexistence in nature.
Each is one of the "Treedom"
series.

Page 107
U.G. Sato

Where can Nature go?
These posters were designed
asking for coexistence in nature.
Each is one of the "Treedom"
series.

Page 108
Wojtek KOREK Korkuć

Papal Day poster, 2006.

Page 109
Isidro Ferrer

Sometimes in the theatre, certain truths appear: metonymy, paradox, synecdoche, ellipsis, quotations, silence, hyperbole, irony, terseness, metaphor, personification, similes and more. They are as true as the day is long. These truths and others are those which appear in this collection of posters thought out and made for the National Dramatic Center; it's logical, a poster for a play needs to present some of the truths that will later appear on stage. We say later because the first thing we see from a play is the poster and while we look at it, we've already started to see the play with the eyes of imagination: the eyes that are born in our throat and look behind only to seem as though they're looking forward.

Page 110
Pekka Loiri

Autumn 2009. Shigeo and I had breakfast together in a small hotel in Mexico City. Soon after I had returned home I got the message about his passing away. I made this Fukuda hommage poster trying to express my great respect and admiration for him, his art and design.

Page 111
Pekka Loiri

Tapani passed away soon after Shigeo's death.
I borrowed the pigeon sitting on the hat from Fukuda's Hommage Poster and placed it in this Aartomaa Poster. The pigeon is a messenger, telling about Tapani's exodus. I showed the pigeon as a cripple, like Tapani was. That disability doesn't bother the pigeon as it never bothered Tapani. Walking might be a bit difficult but they are able to fly.

Page 112
Alain Le Quernec

Shell by shell is about the wreckage of a huge oil tanker on the coast of Bretagne (Brittany) in 1978, creating one of the biggest environmental accidents on the coast of this touristic country.

Page 113
Marlena Buczek

Oil spill, Gulf of Mexico.
The voice of the image extends in diverse ways, becoming the open sound of awareness for a greater cause than one's own personal fulfillment.

Page 114
Uwe Loesch

IQ – poster against radioactive contamination after Tschernobyl.

Page 115
Uwe Loesch

You'll never get that to fit again! For International Congress for industrial health and safety standards.
Trade Fair Düsseldorf.

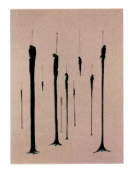

Page 116
Marlena Buczek

Away with green veins, expose
my naked branch and you will
wallow in breathless agony
of pain.

Page 117
Eli Kince

Reign Forest.
The work is meant to be
formally and conceptually
engaging and introspective.
I sought to shift the viewer's
consciousness from their
cognitive thought patterns to
an emotive state.

Page 118
Jochen Fiedler

This poster was shown in 2003
at the International Triennial of
Eco-posters, Kharkov. It was
awarded the Grand Prix at the
Triennale, the fourth block.
The poster appeals to
motorists to respect nature
and its creatures, and to be
considerate when driving.
The illustration shows a car tire,
with the imprints of run-over
animals on the surface.
The colors are limited to black.

Page 119
Yuri Surkov

Alter Eco. Poster for WWF
(World Wildlife Fund for
Nature).

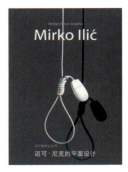

Page 120
Chatri na Ranong

Light Globe.
By breaking existing energy
consumption habits, more
energy efficient technology will
be able to thrive.
Good 50x70.

Page 121
Mirko Ilić

Small Ideas.
The concept behind this is
that a lot of small ideas can
eventually become one big idea.
You never arrive at a big idea at
once, it takes small stages to
eventually build up to it.

Page 122
Mirko Ilić

Cyberhate.
This image was about different
hate/racist groups that took full
advantage of the internet to
propagate their causes.
For example, being lynched
through the internet.

Page 123
Unknown

Against alcoholism.

Page 124
Page Alexander Faldin

Antidrug Poster.

Page 125
Pierre Mendell

Drugs.
Drogen, Initiative of the studio.

Page 126
Kyösti Varis

Your Lifemeter.
Designed to remind us of the dangers of smoking.

Page 127
Kyösti Varis

Your Lifemeter.
Designed to remind us of the dangers of smoking.

Page 128
Alain Le Quernec

Baby doesn't like to smoke.

Page 129
Armando Milani

Smoking is poison.
Hospital Policlinico Milano.

Page 130
Kyösti Varis

This poster encourages road safety.

Page 131
Lex Drewinski

Highway to Disaster, ecological poster.

Page 132
Morteza Momayez

Morteza Momayez exhibition, Saman Gallery.

Page 133
Morteza Momayez

First Asian Graphic Design Biennale.

Page 134
Gunter Rambow

I made posters for the publisher S. Fischer. They were both image posters and also used for the announcement of the spring and autumn collections. The book was shown as a container for philosophy, literature and science.

Page 135
Gunter Rambow

S.Fischer published a wide field of literature since the 1920s. Gerhard Hauptmann, Thomas Mann and Franz Kafka were among their authors. These 2 posters are part of a group of 11 posters that were shown on pillars and boards during the Frankfurt Book Fair from 1976 to 1982.

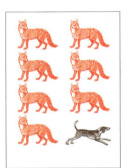

Page 136
Patrick Thomas

Foxes & Hound (after Thomas Bewick).

Page 137
Patrick Thomas

Cock Up.

Page 138
Hilppa Hyrkäs

No European Union, designed for a poster competition organized by Finland's largest newspaper, Helsingin Sanomat.

Page 139
Niklaus Troxler

Switzerland-EU. Switzerland should join the European Union.

Page 140
Massimo Vignelli

Bicentennial poster.
The poster celebrates the
ethnic differences in American
society, against the "melting
pot" theory.

Page 141
Louis Danziger

Exhibition of American
Paintings.
For an exhibition at the Los
Angeles County Museum
of Art.

Page 142
Woody Pirtle

This poster was created
for Pirtle Design as a social
commentary focused on the
financial relationship between
the United States of America
and the People's Republic of
China.

Page 143
Bob Gill

Penguin Press: "American
Capitalism".

Page 144
Maurizio Milani

The other side of energy.
A poster denouncing the role,
sometimes negative, of
energy use.
The electric chair is one of the
most striking metaphors of
this issue.

Page 145
Wojtec KOREK Korkuć

Each authority will be settled.

Page 146
Isidro Ferrer

Truth, lies, and everything else.
50th edition international course
of illustration and graphic design.
Image tribute to Pierre Mendell.

Page 147
Pierre Mendell

As you like it.
Was ihr wollt, Bavarian State
Opera.

Page 148
Ivan Chermayeff

For the UCLA Summer Session
in 2010. Commissed by an
exceptional art director, InJu
Sturgeon, to entice applicants
to go where the sun shines.

Page 149
Michael Mabry

AIGA National Headquaters
Membership poster. American
Institute of Graphic Arts, 2000.

Page 150
Pino Tovaglia

Obligatory circulation.
The Traffic.
Edit by Paolo Bellasich and
Roberto Bossi.

Page 151
Fabrice Praeger

Rainbow wiper. For a street
theater festival in Morocco
called Awalnart, a very new
form of communication for
them: each year, the posters
have a very simple, universal,
joyful, peaceful, poetic, or
surprising visuals.

Page 152
German Montalvo

The image of the poster Tequila
represents a bottle with a
screaming women inside,
graphically combining her
gesture with the word Tequila, a
strong liquor. Ironically, this
is a silent movie that uses only
images.

Page 153
German Montalvo

The postmodernity.
Designed for a sociology
seminar. The image of the
chimpanzee and gorilla alludes
to Darwin's idea that we
all descend from monkeys.
Associating the monkey and
the sociologists as well as the
depiction of the kiss on the
monkey's cheek, are both ways
of poking fun at the sociologists
studying human phenomena.

Page 154
Melchior Imboden

Two of the series of four
silkscreen invitational posters.
Title of the series:
Face to Face.

Page 155
Melchior Imboden

Invitational poster exhibition,
80 photographers and
80 graphic designers from all
over the world.
Gallery Anatome, Paris.

Page 156
Bruno Munari

Picnic.

Page 157
Bruno Munari

La pennellessa.

Page 158
James Cross

"Thinking of You," is a series
of five T-shirt concepts
commissioned by MOCA. We
used various inanimate objects
such as the nut and bolt,
the sun and moon, an angel's
halo and a devil's pitchfork,
each "thinking" of the other for
obvious reasons.

Page 159
James Cross

He asked me to design a
symbol which expressed
the "idea" concept and this is
the result. I developed a series
of these "Thinking of you"
concepts such as a bolt thinking
of a nut.

Page 160
Giulio Confalonieri

For the book series "I Giganti"
published by
Arnoldo Mondadori.

Page 161
Giulio Confalonieri

For the oil tanker Esso
Columbia.

Page 162
George Tscherny

This poster never had words
and is a perfect example of
communication in the Digital
Age, in effect - two graphic
icons talking to each other.

Page 163
George Tscherny

In the beginning was the
Word...
...but, says the French
philosopher Roland Barthes,
"The image always has the last
word", which, as a designer,
I am very much in agreement
with.
School of Visual Arts poster.

Page 164
Paul Rand

Call for entry.

Page 165
James Cross

Design for the call for entries,
for AIGA design competition
where the best graphic design
is awarded.

Page 166
Bob Gill

Illustration:
"Jazz", *Queen Magazine.*

Page 167
Svetlana Faldina
Alexander Faldin

Antiwar poster
"Tempo di marcia".
Notes: Ode to Joy, Beethoven;
Funeral March, Chopin.

Page 168
Milton Glaser

Temple University, Music
Festival / Institute Philadephia.

Page 169
Shigeo Fukuda

The Marriage of Figaro.

Page 170
Armin Hofmann

Poster for a concert in Basler
Gesangverein.

Page 171
Armin Hofmann

Stadt Theater.

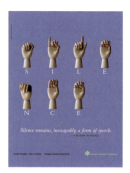

Page 172
Bruno Oldani

Conducting.
Learning Manual.

Page 173
Arnold Schwartzman

"Silence remains, inescapably a
form of speech." Susan Sontag.
The Harold Grinspoon
Foundation.

Page 174
Bruno Monguzzi

Anwesenheit bei Abwesenheit.
Presence of Absence. The
photogram in 20th Century Art".
Kunsthaus, Zurich.

Page 175
Bruno Monguzzi

Le nouveau Salon des Cent.
Ode to the poster designer
Henri de Toulouse-Lautrec for
the centenary of his death,
1901-2001.
A gesture of respect and
generosity from a hundred
poster designers all over the
world.
Toulouse-Lautrec Museum,
Albi.

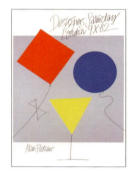

Page 176
Gérard Paris-Clavel

Pedestrian in the city.
This image is about the dilution
of the citizen.
It's a symbol of the alienating
vibrations provoked by the
destructive media and their
omnipresent communication of
insignificant things.

Page 177
Roman Cieslewicz

Poster for the process to Kafka,
from collection of Krzysztof
Dydo. Krakow, Poland.

Page 178
Alan Fletcher
©Raffaella Fletcher

The brief was to produce a
colourful, happy poster to
promote Designers Saturday,
an annual event when classy
furniture manufacturers invite
classy architects and designers
to visit their showrooms.
The intention, while plying them
with food and drink, is to effect
introductions and show off the
latest products.

Page 179
Alan Fletcher
©Raffaella Fletcher

A poster to announce a
retrospective exhibition of 100
posters held at the Design
Museum by G&B Arts, a
London screen printer.
The image is a direct
impression of the colourful right
hand of Alan Fletcher.

Page 180
Wojtec KOREK Korkuć

Advertising poster for
KOREKSTUDIO.

Page 181
Pierre Mendell

The Rape of Lucretia.
Bavarian State Opera.

Page 182
Armando Milani

"Think like a man of action, act
like a man of thought."
Henri Bergson.

Page 183
Ivan Chermayeff

For "Churchill: The Wilderness
Years." The image: Cigar smoke
obliterates the Homburg for a
decade.

Page 184
Patrick Thomas

Kalashnikov/Rickenbacker.

Page 185
Fritz Gottschalk

Classic cases in history and
medicine. George III.
For Roche pharmaceutical
products, symbolising the
Boston Tea-Party and the
fact that George Washington
defeated the British!

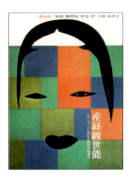

Page 186
Ikko Tanaka

The fifth Sankei Kanze Noh
Performance.

Page 187
Ikko Tanaka

The Winter Olympic Games
in Sapporo '72.

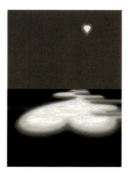

Page 188
Leszek Zebrowski

...I Julietta.

Page 189
Yano Kashimi

My Heart.
Feeling is more important than thinking.

Page 190
Stefano Asili

The Big Bet.
What is the challenge of existence? Is life random? Are our experiences real? Is there a universe around us or do we create its image? And if we really exist, what is death? Only an image? Discontinuity of perception, conscience or of reality? Does God exist? If so, is God a quantum object?

Page 191
Chaz Maviyane-Davies
Paul Peter Piech

"To create is to resist, to resist is to create." Stephane Hessel.

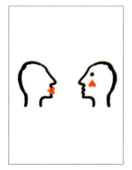

Page 192
Fabrice Praeger

This universal picture was published many times around the world and became very well-known. This image also appeared on a t-shirt for "Monoprix" (very famous shops chain in France) in 2001.

Page 193
Lex Drewinski

Antony and Cleopatra Theater poster.

Page 194
François Robert

These images show conflict, aggression, suffering, and devastation. These images also suggest an aftermath, therefore functioning as a warning.

Page 195
Massimo Dolcini

Resistence for peace against terrorism.
Collection Pierluigi Panzieri.

Posters, at their best, are often very powerful and persuasive communications. A good poster captures the attention of the viewer, that is the first step, but more importantly it engages them.

The poster has proven its value and effectiveness over a very long history, throughout the world. In fact, many of us are moved by posters we see from other countries although we have no understanding of the words. This book gives evidence as to how little the words matter in many posters.

What is it that gives the poster its power?

I believe that comes from the power of the metaphor or symbol, the simple image which can encapsulate complex ideas. An image of a loaf of bread in the hands of a skilled designer can cause one to think of either hunger or, conversely, plenty. It all depends on how the designer uses that image.

By the method of presentation, often through juxtaposition or fusion with other carefully chosen symbols, the poster starts the viewer on a path of interpretation. Ultimately, its message is formed through the mental processes of the viewer. The designer shows A and B but the viewer sees C. It is not A+B = AB which is what the poster actually shows. Rather it is in the viewers mind seen as A+B=C. The answer to the equation takes place in the mind of the viewer, it is that personal involvement that moves him or her.

Louis Danziger / U.S.A.

Written but not spoken
In absence of words they lie

Silent they might be...
Surrounded by white space

By one man composed
And of all

Cheers to Armando Milani

Marlena Buczek / U.S.A.

A poster without words is clear for everybody. It is like a language that is spoken all over the world because they can be understood with heart and mind.

This book contains a very precious collection of loudly speaking and at the same time very silent posters, and here is its value.

Thanks to Mr. Milani for his idea to realize this project.

Faldin Family / Russia

Better Nothing Than Almost.

If we consider posters the underwear of a modern city, then this piece of underwear is without doubt becoming more and more expensive while simultaneously being renewed more and more frequently.
The speed of urban life indulges people with a fickle affection and mentality, and compels people to constantly pursue visual stimuli. "Speed is the form of ecstasy the technical revolution has bestowed on man" (Milan Kundera, *Slowness*). The modern city, of hustle and bustle, of hedonism and decadence, demands the underwear to be sexier and sexier, and more and more exquisite. Consequentially, it is more concerned with the size of posters (the bigger, the better), the saturation of color (the more garish, the better), and the quantity (the more, the better).

The speed of renewal of the underwear is far beyond and detached from the speed of thinking in design, and the phenomenon breeds more designers who are willing to sell their souls, to be subject to the unilateral decisions of clients. Designers nowadays function like a mouse to a computer: they seem intimately associated with design but are, in actuality, never the deciding voice of design. Sympathize with Kundera in *Slowness*: "Why has the pleasure of slowness disappeared? Ah, where have they gone, the amblers of yesteryear? Where have they gone, those loafing heroes of folk song, those vagabonds who roam from one mill to another and bed down under the stars? Have they vanished along the footpaths, with grasslands and clearings, with nature?" *Slowness* induces the unruffled thinking

process, forges elegance, and consummates the work of art.

Posters differ from Fine Art in terms of the accuracy and absoluteness in processing information, but resemble Fine Art in the consensus on the power of imageries.
The creation of graphics can be highly predictive in design, so that the graphics can evoke the anticipated reaction and response from the audience when the audience receives the information. Therefore, in that sense, it has to be exact.
To achieve this exactitude, in most cases, designers seek recourse to texts which embody the precision that graphics cannot acquire. Yet there are also designers who boldly challenge such limitations, and are able to create compelling visual narratives with mere graphics and, in doing so, intentionally obliterate the intervention of text. Their textless graphic posters are oftentimes concise but also extremely striking. This is a Minimalist design approach.

Without the aid of text, designers must exert all their effort to create graphics which deliver an accurate message. To use graphics as an adequate form to narrate text-like content without being too dreary is indeed a challenge, and in fact, we can barely find a handful of successful pieces. However, *No Words Posters* by Armando Milani is a rarity that assembles many outstanding exemplars.

I would like to express my sincere gratitude to his quiet contribution in the era of high-speed and cacophony.

Jianping He / Germany

Many poster designs mingle text and images or use text only to communicate the message. However, it's rare to see a poster that does not include words, and even less common to find a book that specially address on design of the "image only" posters.
It's well known that images appeared earlier than words in prehistoric communication. Today, it's said, "a picture is worth a thousand words." This is true, especially as the world moves closer to McLuhan's global village. As new technology and media allow ease of international communication, design issues become a shared, worldwide experience. When seen in this light, "no words" poster designs could surmount language barriers and boost international communications and understanding. Furthermore, it's very common that posters propose questions and answer their own questions with convincing text and images. This approach is straightforward and easy to understand for an audience that shares the same language and culture. However, posters with appropriate imagery as the only visual element reach a much broader audience, regardless of language and culture differences, because they are less specific - leaving room for the audience to fill in the meanings based on their own contexts and experiences.
Armando Milani's book will deepen and further the research into the design of this unique genre of poster. I believe research on designing posters without words will not only explore the universal language potential further, but also likely open new directions for contemporary visual communication designs. This is where the book's value lies.

Fang Chen / China / U.S.A.

Dear Armando,

Fabrice.

Fabrice Praeger / France

A poster without words is like poetry. Concentrated, suggestive and closest to art.

A wordless work can easily become a very powerful icon that has the qualities to last in the pantheon of visuals, and becomes an international asset.

Because of the fact that no words are involved, the poster must be minimalistic, pure and very communicative on one hand, and very direct on the other hand, using basic metaphors which are similar to road signs. No wonder some of the works shown in this collection can have strong impact in the streets.

Another significant feature of this special collection is the arrangement of the works done by Armando Milani which creates in each double spread, sometimes connected visually and sometimes by the content, another wonderful connection, and in each one, another beautiful story is born.

Yossi Lemel / Israel

In a world of Tweets, Likes, Follows, Pins etc... of visual confusing messages and "cut and paste", Armando Milani's book reaffirms once again what Federico Fellini once said "If there were a little more silence, if we all kept quiet...maybe we could understand something." From this book we all understand the power of great images and what strong visual messages can achieve... in silence.

Ezio Burani / Italy

Posters are most often a combination of visual and verbal metaphors which, if successful, play off each other.

Unfortunately, too often the two are either simply redundant or have no intelligent connection at all. Armando has proven that the most powerful, most explicit expressions can be visual alone, without the verbal at all.

The "no words posters" allow for personal interpretation of the conceptual visual metaphor which is far more memorable than visual content, explained by a headline from someone else's point of view.

James Cross / U.S.A.

The language of modern posters is specific, short, immediate and strong. The perfect poster combines the visual language of the image and the typographic message of the text. The text modifies and amplifies the image as much as the image synthesizes/interprets the meaning of the words. This combination makes the mystery and the art of the poster.

For technical reasons, before the 20th century, posters were only textuals, afterwards, for economical reasons, these textual posters always existed and they still exist especially with the art of typography.

But textless posters are as rare as the flying fish, they exist but they are not the majority of the species. The messages are obvious, some are primary, others like Uwe Loesch's works, subtle and corrosive.

Some are unforgettable, like Fukuda's canon, a reference in the history of posters. Some of the posters presented here have minimal words that have been omitted for the purpose of the book, with the consent of the artist. These texts are not a part of a composition, they are titles for paintings, written as discreetly as a signature.

Timeless and powerful, naked raw communication.

Alain Le Quernec / France

The value of design builds on inspiration and the creation of eternality.

Graphic Design does not only deal with the communication of information, but also reflects current social events, concerns society and environment and inspires humanity. Global warming is a critical issue nowadays. It is an issue tightly linked with the environment, ecology and the subsistence of human being.

Our mother earth has sent out the warning signals. Global warming is one of them. Increasing temperature results in sea level rise. These sea level rises could lead to potentially catastrophic difficulties for shore-based communities. Some island nations would be submerged if the sea level is high enough.

I am trying to reveal this environmental issue in my work. I hope this work will appeal to everyone to take care of our environment and love this planet we are living on.

Leo Lin / Taiwan

In today's digital era, so much culture comes to us through a computer screen.

We are drowned in email blasts and web pages, and it seems that poster art has lost its importance as a communicative tool. But posters live in theaters and clubs and political rallies, places where real people meet other real people. And I believe we need that human connection even more, now that we're in such a virtual world.

Critics often do not qualify posters as high art. While this is a good subject for an argument, art is not a definition, it is an experience. If a poster moves you and makes you think, then it doesn't matter how a critic would label it. It is art with a capital "A," art that is able to spark change.

Luba Lukova / U.S.A.

Thank you Armando, for creating this book. A real book, real paper, that sets down the memory of the world's emotions on that material that graphic designers love so much. A book that is not afraid of time, unlike the digital media that become oblivious to any change in an operating system. A paper book made of paper pages that represent paper objects. It speaks— and teaches you to think— like a book for children who cannot yet read. Many years from now, my children will be able to leaf through it, but they might not be able to do the same with my computer. Being included in this book is a privilege and a great honor.

Stefano Asili / Italy

There are posters which convey a clear message, where there is no shadow of doubt, whether or not they include text.

For more sophisticated and ambiguous that the image articulation can be—and the mastery of graphic language—inks, shapes and colors take possession of the generous paper surface that receives them, leaving a definitive, irreversible mark.

I have always been impressed by the ability that the poster has to work with so many issues in synthetic and personal ways, where the artist's style is not felt as a trap but as something that frees.

This reflection confronts us with what I consider a main challenge, and consequently creative stimuli: the balance between freedom and limits.

I think it is that friction which generates the great energy of the poster and which makes it so universal: to show that with a few notes one can make a symphony.

Rico Lins / Brazil

A good poster conveys messages effectively, and presents them esthetically to the viewer. Its objective is to lure, to sell, to inform, to invite, to command, to guide and to teach, to convince, to appeal and to manipulate. It is far more than merely a notice or an announcement in a frame.

Depending on the situation, a poster might whisper or call. It screams, stamps, whistles at beautiful women or throws stones through windows. Its function is to present information. In order to be able to tell its news, it first of all has to be recognized.

Ideally, an illustration does not require its beholder to speak the language. Posters work by making a Japanese tourist who doesn't speak French interested in a Grand Opéra show, or by encouraging people to think of the consequences of global warming. The stories told on posters are never exhausted – only the way they are told depends on the author, time and target audience.

A good poster is so much more than just a brutal picture that merely intends to startle. This sort of shock tactic is violating and offensive.

When esthetics are lost and all that remains is brutality, we will certainly stop, but it will leave a sour taste.
And this is the ruthlessness in designing a good poster: how do you combine elegance, civilized behavior and refinement with the effective delivery of messages?
How can you be gracious and defiant, esthetic and sinful all at the same time?

A good poster opens up pictorially.
A poster's typography is like a spice— a frequent key and interesting aspect of the overall graphics and composition.

However, the essential function of typography is to inform us when and where a circus gives its performance or where to meet in order to make the world a better place.

Loiri Pekka / Finland

Feeling is more important than Thinking. I always care about creating emotional expression which is aimed at the subconscious minds of the audience.

If there is no word in front of you, there is only that which you feel. I believe that sometimes "No Word" can say more, and more directly, than a long sentence, even if we don't have any common language.

I am glad to have this opportunity. Because, my artwork "My Heart" with no words has been selected by a man who doesn't speak the same language that I do.
I am really happy to join this project.
Thank you so much, Armando.

Kashimi Yano / Japan

A great poster is somewhat like the wink of an eye.

With a succinct, thoughtful gesture, a skilled designer is capable of communicating a sometimes complicated message within an instant.

That's really all the time one has to capture the attention of the passerby on the sidewalk, in a taxi, or on the subway.

The challenge is to cement quickly the connection with the audience and tell a story that's often much deeper than what it appears to be on the surface.

A master poster designer must also be a master of distillation, using all the tools available to create a poster that is simple, direct, and easy to comprehend. A poster that is iconic and communicative, with minimum means, is a confirmation of the mantra that less is more.

This book showcases a collection of posters that speak to us loud and clear... without saying a word.

Woody Pirtle / U.S.A.

The human skeleton is a powerful visual symbol. It's come to represent the "remains", what's left after life has ended, after the flesh and mind cease to function. In my photographs, I use the human skeleton as the formal visual element, the subject of the image.

In this manner, the skeleton is both the protagonist and antagonist (the Buddhist notion about, "the duality of man" seems apt).

For each photograph, I disassemble the modular system of the skeleton and reconfigure the elements to form a new image. These images are man-made.

Images of aggression, images that cause suffering, devastation and conflict. I intend the images to plant the notion of restraint and charity in an effort to promote peace and tolerance.

François Robert / U.S.A.

I grew up in Switzerland at a time when posters were an extremely important means of communication. I even peeled and stole some of them right off the poster columns. Posters by Armin Hofmann, Celestino Piatti, Herbert Leupin, Herbert Matter, Joseph Müller-Brockman, and later Wolfgang Weingart, Werner Jekker, Ralph Schraivogel and others were enriching the environment. Those single image expressions were the reason I became a graphic designer.

Unfortunately, we in the USA no longer have a poster culture, mainly because there is no place to display them, and therefore no client is asking for it. Words have become more important, especially in advertising, and the image has become just an illustration of what the words already say.
A clever headline seems to be more important then a visually arresting image.

This book is the essence of pure visual communication. The designer is expressing the idea with an absolute minimum of means, making it all the more powerful, because the viewer is participating in completing the image with meaning.

Thank you, Armando, for showing us that this visual language is still spoken loudly all over the world.

Steff Geissbühler / U.S.A.

Despite the power of words, there are inevitable instances when ideas cannot be properly expressed when words are translated from one language to the next.

The strength in these posters is that their messages remain undiluted by the process of translation.

Their symbolic nature allows a universal audience to interpret and understand complex ideas in ways that may not have been possible with words alone.

Chatri na Ranong / Australia

Not a word, all visual posters!
That's ideal, full of visual language.
I always challenged but failed.
My dream poster is yet to be a reality. Soon!

U.G. Sato / Japan

As the proverb goes "A picture's meaning can express ten thousand words", likewise, in Armando's comprehensive book, *No Words Posters*, "180 pictures are worth ten thousand words".

Growing up in England, I recall a War Office poster "Your talk may kill your comrades", by my friend and mentor Abram Games. It displayed an image of a vortex winding out of a soldier's mouth, its extremity becomes a bayonet skewering his comrades.
The message was so clear it made the copy redundant.

Games' maxim was "Maximum Meaning Minimum Means".

Designers often feel that putting words to pictures merely becomes a form of tautology; regrettably we are often slaves to our clients' demands.

On examining the majority of the posters in this book, I found it interesting to note that the majority of the images were not only sans words but also sans clients! Because the client is humanity.

In reference to my own poster in this book, my concept is a visual interpretation of a quotation by Susan Sontag, "Silence remains, inescapably, a form of speech," a quotation that I felt required no words, thus I chose to spell out the word "silence" in sign language for the deaf.

Arnold Schwartzman / U.S.A.

It's normal that the verbiage on a poster provides a context for the image or vice versa. The posters in Armando Milani's remarkable compilation of what he has dubbed *No Words Posters* are different. Words, and all that is not essential, have been stripped away.

These posters are confrontational and enigmatic. They're contentious, and immediately bypass the brain to pound directly on the guts, or pull at the heartstrings, of an audience that normally relies on the verbal context to tune them into the nuances of meaning.

Consistently, these images flow naturally from ideas that sprout directly from the human condition, and their creators are much more than talented image-makers; they're anthropologists with their fingers on mother earth's pulse.

Lanny Sommese / U.S.A.

Since thousands of years ago, man could receive and understand pictorial messages better and faster than verbal messages. Cavemen believed in the magic of the picture, so by illustrating their desires on cave walls, they inscribed and left them to posterity.

Nowadays in graphic design works, especially in the field of the social posters, the power of the image still predominates that of the writing. Pictorial messages are quicker than writing in creating excitement in the audiences, and are more memorable.

Wordless posters are not mere photos or illustrations, but frames that designers have chosen to convert to icons to instill in the minds of their audiences. There are posters that speak a thousand words without any title or motto. It is interesting that when looking at the posters in this book, one reaches the conclusion that most successful posters that somehow rub shoulders with art have not been designed with current trends or fashions in mind. They have originated at the bottoms of the souls of their designers.

As ever, Armando Milani is the sharp hunter of creative themes and ideas. This time he has come up with the idea of the *No Words Posters* book from the heart of the graphic artists' works. He has presented the posters with his no-words filter. Not even the designers themselves had ever looked at their own works in his way.

Parisa Tashakori / Iran

This book contains some fantastic images. I think design is the new art.

Seeing these posters with their text messages removed makes them strangely reminiscent of New York's poster scene. Unlike Europe where the poster tradition is kept alive by the existence of free-standing advertising columns, American cities provide no such 'civilized' opportunity for the display of commercial, political or cultural posters.

Here buildings, sidewalks and construction sites are an endless canvas for the unsanctioned mounting of posters and art. The result is an uncontrolled urban art where the boundary between street and gallery art is often blurred.
It is also transient—but so is life.

George Tscherny / U.S.A.

I love the idea of Armando's Milani book.

His selection shows that the visual language is a universal and timeless tool enabling communication beyond divisions present in the contemporary world.

When I look at this book, I have no doubts that it is possible to convey an intriguing and "silent" message concerning any matter or emotion – by using a dominant and precise statement, provoking discussion or allowing freedom of interpretation and space for one's own reflection.

The book represents important matters and it is beautiful. Thank you, Armando.

Monika Zawadzki / Poland

With every design solution, the combination of one image and the next, or between image and text, generates new metaphors. In this sense, it is unusual to communicate without words.

When doing so, however, it is worth noting that every cultural group is subject to its own language conventions.

Which means that designing text involves more idiosyncratic (rather than universally comprehensible—i.e. extending beyond cultural boundaries) image design.

2xGoldstein / Switzerland

This wonderful book created by Armando should be mandatory reading for all graphic design students.

In time of Twitter, Flickr and Spotify, we graphic designers have to fight for our place in the sun.

Young designers in the digital age are reluctant to listen to us 'old guys' when we preach that the idea is king – and not the medium by which it is delivered.

This collection of simple ideas and powerful visuals shows that true social media is a graphic with a message. #Hashtags, Upload and Invite Friends betray us all.

Garth Walker / South Africa

In today's world of too much hot air, already the title *No Words* is mightily recommendable.
Short: a great idea!

A wonderful *contrapunto* to today's mental and visual pollution.
What a great challenge to get an idea across, in a creative, concise, refreshing, sometimes even witty way.

Thank you, Armando, for compiling such a wonderful oeuvre.
And the book is, of course, well designed and produced! A gem to possess and cherish.

Fritz Gottschalk / Switzerland

Every unprecedented poster carries with it the dream of existing as a work of art. What all began in the days of Toulouse-Lautrec remains the declared or unacknowledged dream of every poster designer still today: creating a work that not only manages to be put on display in public space, but also succeeds in one of the numerous international poster competitions and finds entrance into the renowned poster collections of international museums and private collections.

Today's mass of designs in the field, however, warrants the question of what makes a good poster. The challenge of a good design entails a creative act which contributes to personal development, raises the viewer's consciousness, and prompts an active analysis of a specific aspect of our environment.

But a poster does not define itself solely in an economical, political or cultural context. It must also be capable of standing its ground over the course of time.
Found time and again in leading collections and major international museums are posters whose use of forms have borne a universal significance and whose messages have withstood the test of time, works we look upon as great design to this day.

We are called upon to demonstrate to the young generation that within the broad spectrum of poster design, far beyond all the neon and streetlights, there are also stars which show themselves in the sky because of their significance, and serve as better navigation aids and references in meeting the challenges.

Unarguably, posters will have new and different platforms in the future. Perhaps their ubiquity will have an even more annoying or disturbing effect on the everyday lives of viewers as an irruptive medium. But poster design will – as it has for more than two hundred years – continue to face the same challenge of getting its message across to the viewer. This is the economic imperative. And conveying it as lastingly as possible – this is the aesthetic imperative.

Armando Milani has succeeded in selecting from a myriad of existing posters a small number of works which manage without words, and thus carry an important and lasting message out into the world.

Melchior Imboden / Switzerland

Armando Milani is not a person of many words. He is a real gentleman designer, with great respect for his colleagues´ work. What I can say is that this is not at all typical. Most designers never tire of talking about their own experiences.

No wonder Armando Milani started collecting posters without words from his friends and colleagues all over the world. This is fantastic: to dialogue with colleagues— that´s culture!

I remember Armando´s early book project, entitled *Double Life*, in which he presented his AGI colleagues on one side in a funny way and on the other side in a serious way. To present posters without words is again a remarkable project.
As designers we always try to transform contents by pure visual expression.

And we all know how ambitious this can be. To discover so many strong solutions in one book is a great pleasure. Graphic Design as an international language, understandable all over the world – how fantastic!

Niklaus Troxler / Switzerland

Sometimes words diminish the visual. Sometimes words amplify the visual. It´s always good to be able to tell the difference.

Milton Glaser / U.S.A.

Extremism in design works. No words work. All words work.

Stefan Sagmeister / U.S.A.

Armando always comes up with great ideas for his books which are always beautifully designed, and this one is clearly no exception.

What could be more perfect than pictures with no words to a visual community?

B. Martin Pedersen / U.S.A.

Once again Armando Milani has composed a poem without words.

A master of the lyrical approach in communication, Armando has applied his sharp eye and sensitive mind to select the work of his peers, a collection of posters without words.

If Art is useful and Design is utilitarian, these posters transcend their utilitarian side to reach the sublime, often reserved for Art.

This book is a great tool for the younger generation to understand the power of this medium when supported by intelligence and sense, even without words.

Massimo Vignelli / U.S.A.

Last Words.

There are posters with strong visual messages and deadly boring headlines. They are killing themselves softly.

There are posters with intelligent headlines and stupid images. They are awfully successful.

There are posters with an ingenious realationship between headlines and images. They are once in a blue moon.

There are posters with identical visual and verbal messages. They are dead-and-alive.

There are posters with persuasive headlines only. They provoke the image in the head and inspire the imagination.

And there are posters without words. They are sometimes inspirational and easy to read by illiterates in the global village.

Uwe Loesch / Germany

Index

Addresses

Mehmet Ali Turkmen
Cihangir Caddesi 38/3
Cihangir, Beyoglu
34433 Istanbul, Turkey
Phone: +90 212 292 27 62
mat@matistanbul.net
www.matistanbul.net

Robert Appleton
861-55 Dalhousie Street
Toronto M5B2P7. Canada
Phone: +41645 786 06
bob@robertappleton.com
www.robertappleton.com

Katsumi Asaba
3-9-2 Minami-Aoyama
Minato-ku, Tokyo
107-0062. Japan
Phone: +81 3 3479 0471
Fax: +81 3 3402 0694
aoki@asaba-d.co.jp
www.asaba-design.com

Stefano Asili
Via Ponchielli 33
I - 09129 Cagliari
Sardinia, Italy
Phone: +39 070 480248
Mobile: +39 347 0800805
stefano.asili@gmail.com
www.asilieboassa.com
www.asi.li

Anthon Beeke
Hortusplantsoen 6
Amsterdam, 1018. TZ
Phone: +31 20 528 70 14
anthon@beeke.nl

Pierre Bernard
Atelier de creation graphique
220, rue du faubourg
Saint Martin.
75010 Paris, France
Phone: +33(0)1 4038 6686
pierre.bernard@acgparis.com
www.acgparis.com

Marlena Buczek
Marlena Buczek Smith
Wallington NJ, USA
www.marlenabuczek.com
marlenabuczek@yahoo.com

Stephan Bundi
Schloss-Strasse 78
CH-3067 Boll/Bern
Switzerland
Phone: +41 31 981 00 55
info@atelierbundi.ch
www.atelierbundi.ch

Ezio Burani
QNY Creative
1181 Broadway, 8 fl.
New York, NY 10001
www.qnycreative.com

Ken Carbone
22 West 19th St, 10th Floor
New York, NY 10011. USA
Phone: +1 212 807 0011
Fax: +1 212 807 0870
ken@carbonesmolan.com
www.carbonesmolan.com

Ivan Chermayeff
137 East 25 Street
New York, New York 10010
USA
Phone: +1 212 532 4595
info@cgstudionyc.com

James Cross
Napa Valley, California
USA
Phone: +1 707 967 8113
Fax: +1 707 967 9967
jimcross26@gmail.com
jamesacross@sbcglobal.net

Louis Danziger
Arcadia
CA 91066-0189. USA
Phone: +1 626 446 7717
loudanz@earthlink.net

Lex Drewinski
Prof. Dr. habil. Lex Drewinski
Rheinstr. 74
14612 Falkensee /b. Berlin
Germany
Phone: +49 3322 241 336
DrewinskiLexi@aol.com
www.lexdrewinski.com

Alexander and Alexandra Faldin
Phone: +7 812 4611985
Mobile: +7 911 2573392
www.faldin.ru

Svetlana Faldina
fchenpsu@gmail.com
196655, Saint-Petersburg,
Kolpino, ul.
Truda, d. 15/5, kv. 2
Russia

Raffaella Fletcher
Merrilies
Woodcote Road
Forest Row
East Sussex RH 185 AP UK

Fang Chen
919 Stratford Court.
State College
PA 16801 USA
Phone: +1 757 215-5689

Isidro Ferrer
Plaza de Justicia 1. bajo
22001 Huesca, Spain
Phone: +34 97 422 87 32
isidroferrer@telefonica.net
www.isidroferrer.com

Jochen Fiedler
Grafikdesigner
Deutschland
04105 Leipzig
Friedrich-Ebert-Straße 122
damm-fiedler@t-online.de

Steff Geissbühler
60 Hollywood Drive
Hastings-on-Hudson
NY 10706
USA
Phone: +1 914 478 4095
steff@geissbuhler.com
www.geissbuhler.com

Bob Gill
One 5 th Avenue
New York, N.Y. 10003
USA
bobgilletc@nyc.rr.com

Milton Glaser
207 East 32nd Street
New York, NY 10016.
USA
Phone: +1 212 889 3161
Fax: +1 212 213 4072
milton@miltonglaser.com
www.miltonglaser.com

2XGOLDSTEIN
Am Hang 26
76287 Rheinstetten
Deutschland
T 0049 7242 95 39 635
M 0049 171 53 33 052
mail@2xgoldstein.de
www.2xgoldstein.de

Fritz Gottschalk
Boecklinstrasse 26
8032 Zurich, Switzerland
Phone: +47 44 382 18 50
mail@gottashzrh.com

Jianping He
Hesign International GmbH
Hektorstr, 3
D-10711 Berlin. Germany
Phone: +49 30 4508 6575
studio@hesign.com
www.hesign.com

Fons Hickmann
Mariannenplatz 23
10997 Berlin, Germany
Phone: +49 30 69518501
m23@fonshickmann.com
www.m23.de

Armin Hofmann
Museggstrasse 28
Luzern, 6004 CH.
Phone: +41 41 410 62 71

Hilppa Hyrkäs
Rackersinkatu 13
10300 Raseborg
Finland
Phone: +358 40 7556 319
design@hilppahyrkas.fi
www.hilppahyrkas.fi

Mirko Ilić
207 e 32nd street
New York NY 10016 USA
Phone: +1 212 481 9737
Fax: +1 212 481 7088
studio@mirkoilic.com
www.mirkoilic.com

Melchior Imboden
Eggertsbühl
6374 Buochs
Switzerland
mail@melchiorimboden.ch
www.melchiorimboden.ch

Werner Jeker
Les Ateliers du Nord
Place du Nord 2
Ch 1005 Lausanne
Switzerland
Phone: +41 21 320 58 08
Fax: +41 21 320 58 43

Alexander Jordan
ble.org
28 Rue Planchat
Paris, 75020. France
Phone: +33 1 40 09 61 50
Fax: +33 1 40 09 61 55
nte@wanadoo.fr
www.noustravaillonsensem

Sadik Karamustafa
Asmalimescit Sehbender
Sokak 4/5
Beyoglu Tunel 34430
Istanbul, Turkey
Phone: +90 212 251 50 91
Fax: +90 212 251 52 11
Mobile: 0532 523 92 45
sadikkaramustafa@gmail.com
karamustafas@tnn.net

Yano Kashimi
Terashima Design Co.
3rd floor, Iwasa Bldg, Kita 3.
Higashi5. Chuo-ku.
Sapporo, Hokkaido
060-0033 Japan
Phone: 81 11 241 6018
yano@tera-d.net
www.tera-d.net

Eli Kince
Kince Inc / Eli Kince Art Gallery
415 west 146 street
New York NY 10031-5204
U.S.A.
Phone: +1 212 281 7493
Fax: +1 212 281 7290
info@kince.com
www.kince.com

Wojtek KOREK Korkuć
ul. Sulejkowska 60B lok. 601
04-157 Warsaw, POLAND
Phone: +48 601 20 96 31
+48 603 05 67 88
korek@korekstudio.com.pl
www.korekstudio.com.pl

Henrik Kubel
Unit G3, 35-42 Charlotte Road
London.
EC2A 3PD, GB.
Phone: +44 20 7739 4249
henrik@a2swhk.co.uk
www.a2swhk.co.uk

Guillaume Lanneau
63 rue de la Division du
Général Leclerc
94110 Arcueil - France
Phone: +33 0687208750
glanneau@free.fr

Yossi Lemel
3 Hamelakha st.Tel Aviv
P.o.b. 51382. 67215
Mobile: +972 054 5360151
Phone: +972 03 7616700
Fax: +972 03 7616701
yossilemel@hotmail.com
lemel@lemel-cohen.co.il
www.lemel.co.il

Alain Le Quernec
27 Rue du Moulin aux Couleurs
Quimper, 29000. France
Phone: +33 2 98 95 61 76
alain.lequernec@wanadoo.fr
www.alainlequernec.fr

Leo Lin
11F. No.64. Ln. 700
Zhongzheng Rd Xindian Dist.
New Taipei City 231
Taiwan (R.O.C.)

Rico Lins
Rua Campevas 617 - Perdizes
CEP 05016-010 Sao Paulo SP
Brasil
Phone 55 11 3675.3507
rico@ricolins.com
www.ricolins.com

Uwe Loesch
Prof. Uwe Loesch
Arbeitsgemeinschaft
fur visuelle und verbale
Kommunication
Diepensiepen 50
40822 Mettmann, Germany
Phone: +49 2104 806112
contact@uweloesch.de
www.uweloesch.de

Pekka Loiri
Original Loiri Oy
Selkamerenk 7 C 43
00180 Helsinki, Finland
design@originalloiri.fi
www.originalloiri.fi

Luba Lukova
3105 Crescent Street
Suite A Long Island City
NY 1106. USA
Phone: 718 956 1045
luba@lukova.net
www.lukova.net
www.clayangold.com

Michael Mabry
4238 Halleck Street
Emeryville, CA 94608. USA
Phone: +1 510 985 0750
Fax: +1 510 985 0753
E michael@michaelmabry.com
www.michaelmabry.com

Federica Marangoni
Fedrastudiodesign
Dorsoduro 2615
30123 Venezia
www.federicamarangoni.com
www.fedrastudiodesign.com

Chaz Maviyane-Davies
247 Garden St. Apt. 10
Cambridge , Ma 02138-1252
U.S.A.
Phone: +617 547 5292
chazmaviyane@gmail.com

Armando Milani
Via Lambro 7, 20129
Milano, Italy
Phone: +39 0276022468
Mobile: +39 348 3036727
armandomilani@milanidesign.it

Maurizio Milani
Via Bramante 43,
20154 Milano, Italy
Phone: +39 0276022468
Mobile: +39 3299436746
info@milanidesign.it

Bruno Monguzzi
Salita Francesco Melchioni 5
6866 Meride,Switzerland.
phone: +41 91 646 61 07
bruno@monguzzi.ch

Germán Montalvo
Anganguan 20-B
Conjunto Momoxpan
San Pedro Cholula
Puebla 72770
México
Phone: +52 222 231 7493
elchicodelamoto@yahoo.com

Chatri na Ranong
Flat 19
1 Carney Place
London SW9 8GE
United Kingdom
Mobile: +44 7979 862 632
anything@chatri.com.au

Bruno Oldani
Bygday Alle 28B. N-0265
Oslo, Norway
Phone: +47 22 12 84 70
bruno@oldanidesign.no
www.oldanidesign.no

Sergio Olivotti
Gradinata delle Rose, 8
17024 Finale Ligure
Italy
Phone: +39 3389185170
www.olivotti.it
sergioolivotti@icloud.com

Gérard Paris-Clavel
11 Place Voltaire
94200 Ivry-sur-Seine
France

B. Martin Pedersen
389 5th Ave
Suite 1105
New York, NY 10016 USA
Phone: +212 532-9387
perry@graphis.com

Kari Piippo
Katajamäenkatu 14
50170 Mikkeli. Finland
Phone: +358 15 162 187
Fax: +358 15 16 26 87
kari@piippo.com
www.piippo.com/kari

Woody Pirtle
89 Church Hill Road
New Paltz, New York
Phone: 845 6583908
woody@pirtledesign. com

Fabrice Praeger
54 bis, rue de l'Ermitage.
75020 Paris. France
Phone: +33 (0)1 40 33 17 00
fabrice.praeger@Wanadoo.fr

Gunter Rambow
Galerie, Domplatz 16
18273 Gustrom
Germany

François Robert
4835 North Via Chapo
Tucson Arizona 85718
USA

Raban Ruddigkeit
ruddigkeit corporate ideas
Anklamer Straße 32, 10115
Berlin, Germany
Phone: 49 (0)30 80 92 97 77
Mobile: +49 (0)173 5 63 40 91
raban@ruddigkeit.de
www.ruddigkeit.de

John Rushworth
11 Needham Road
London
W11 2RP. United Kingdom
Phone: +44 207 229 3477
Fax: +44 207 727 9932
rushworth@pentagram.co.uk
www.pentagram.com

Stefan Sagmeister
206 West 23rd Street
New York 10011 USA
Phone: 212 647 1789
stefan@sagmeister.com
www.sagmeister.com

Koichi Sato
4-12-16-402 Hongo
Bunkyo-ku, Tokyo
113-0033. Japan
Phone: ++81 3 5804 7655
Fax: +81 3 5804 7656

U.G. Sato
Design Farm Inc. 75 Yaraicho
Shinjuku-ku, Tokyo
ugsato@kt.rim.or.jp
www.ugsato.com
Japan 162-0805
Phone: +81 3267 1267

Arnold Schwartzman
317 1/2 N. Sycamore Avenue
Los Angeles, CA 90036, USA
Phone: 323 938 1481
arnold@schwartzmandesign.
com

Lanny Sommese
100 Rose Drive
Port Matilda, PA 16870, USA
Phone: +1 814 880 8143
lxs14@psu.edu
www.sommesedesign.com

Yuri Surkov
Shturvalnaya 3-2-381.
125363, Moscow, Russia
Phone/Fax: +714951 492 1591
suric@tushino.com

Parisa Tashakori
No.9, 3rd Floor, Suite 8/3,
Khoie Alley, Shariati St.
Tehran 1661714149, Iran
info@parisatashakori.com
www.parisatashakori.com

Patrick Thomas
Studio laVista
Passaige de Masoliver 25-27
08005 Barcelona, Spain
Phone: +34 933 208 114
info@patrickthomas.com
www.patrickthomas.com

Niklaus Troxler
Bahnhofstrasse 22
Willisau, Switzerland
6130, CH
Phone +41 41 970 27 31
Fax: +41 041 970 32 31
E troxler@troxlerart.ch
www.troxlerart.ch

George Tscherny
238 East 72 Street
New York N.Y. 10021, USA
Phone: +1 212 734 3277
gtscherny@aol.com

Herman Van Bostelen
Breedstraat 9A,3512 TS
Utrecht, The Netherlands
Phone: +31 30 223 14 24
info@hermanvanbostelen,nl.

Kyösti Varis
Rauhalanpuisto 10 B 35
02230 Espoo. Finland
Phone:+358 50 570 4588
kyosti.varis.orig@kolumbus.fi
www.varisoriginal.fi

Pasquale Volpe
PVOLPEDESIGN
via Malaga 6, 20143
Milano, Italy.
Phone: +39 02 89159685
Fax: +39 02 89159686
design1@pvolpedesign.com
pvolpedesign.com

Garth Walker
Mister Walker
33 Churchill Road Stamford Hill
Durban 4001 South Africa
PO box 51289 Musgrave Road
KZN 4062 South Africa
Phone: +27 31 312 0572
Mobile: +27 83 637 3636
garth@misterwalker.net
misterwalker.net
garthwalkerphotography.com

David Wang Xingong
2fl. No.195 Chien-kuo South
Road Sec.2 Taipei
Taiwan, China
Phone: +886 2 27080389
wang.desg@msa.hinet.net

Monika Zawadzki
ul. Lechicka 6/9
02-156 Warsaw
Poland

Leszek Zebrowski
Wilkow Marsich 5am6
71-063 Szczecin, Poland
Phone: +48 535 474 740
zebrowskileszek@gmail.com
www.zebrowski-poster.com
www.zebrowski.dphoto.com

Designers who passed away:

Tapani Aartomaa
Finland / 2009

Masuteru Aoba
Japan / 2011

Franco Balan
Italy / 2013

Roman Cieslewicz
Poland / 1996

Giulio Confalonieri
Italy / 2008

Massimo Dolcini
Italy / 2005

Alan Fletcher
UK / 2006

Shigeo Fukuda
Japan / 2009

Yusaku Kamekura
Japan / 1997

Lele Luzzati
Italy / 2007

Pierre Mendell
Germany / 2008

Morteza Momayez
Iran / 2005

Bruno Munari
Italy / 1998

Paul Rand
USA / 1996

Albe Steiner
Italy / 1974

Ikko Tanaka
Japan /2002

Pino Tovaglia
Italy / 1977

Maciej Urbaniec
Poland / 2004

Massimo Vignelli
USA / 2014

Thanks

I would like to thank all the designers that participated in the creation of this book by generously offering their designs and their time, answering my many questions and requests. They have all helped to create this precious collection.

Thanks to this project I have made many new friends from all the parts of the world.

In particular I would like to thank those designers who provided their impressions about the book, helping to clarify the intent and the spirit of this project.

Thanks to Aoi Kono Huber and Aia Tanaka for helping me to contact the Japanese design community.

Thanks to the publisher of the books *50X70*, and *One by One* that allowed me to discover many new talented designers.

I would like to thank Sergio Noberini, director of the Museo Luzzati in Genoa, for organizing an exhibition and an event in Genoa for the promotion of this project.

I also want to thank Francesco Briganti, who patiently assisted me throughout the endless changes to the design of the book.

Armando Milani

Every effort has been made to trace the original source of copyright material contained in this book.
The publisher would be pleased to hear from copyright holders to rectify any error or omission.

The variation in image quality within this publication is due to the fact that some images have been taken from books and not from the original artwork.
Their lack of quality in no way reflects the original works.

Colophon

Printed and bound by:
Jostens Book Manufacturing
Clarksville, TN, USA

Paper:
100# McCoy Silk Text

Typeface:
Univers designed by Adrian Frutiger

This book was made possible, in part, through
the generosity of Mark and Maura Resnick.